A STUDY IN SOUTHSEA

The New Doctor. An early and rare photograph showing the young Doctor Conan Doyle relaxing outside his home at No 1 Bush Villas, Elm Grove, Southsea. On the left is his doctor's red lamp, and at right, fixed to the railings, his brass plate. (Photo: courtesy of Mr Richard Lancelyn Green).

A STUDY IN SOUTHSEA

THE UNREVEALED LIFE
OF
DOCTOR
ARTHUR CONAN DOYLE

Geoffrey Stavert

MILESTONE PUBLICATIONS

Published by Milestone Publications
62 Murray Road, Horndean
Portsmouth, Hants PO8 9JL

Design Brian Iles

Typeset by The Monitor, Hayling Island, Hampshire.

Printed and bound in Great Britain by
R.J. Acford, Industrial Estate, Chichester, Sussex

British Library Cataloguing in Publication Data
Stavert, Geoffrey
  A Study in Southsea : the unrevealed
  life of Dr. Arthur Conan Doyle.
  1. Doyle, *Sir*, Arthur Conan——Biography
  2. Authors, English——19th century——
  Biography
  I. Title
  823'.912   PR4623

  ISBN 0·903852·92·6

Sources and Acknowledgements

I HAVE TRIED as far as possible to go back to primary sources, namely Conan Doyle's autobiography *Memories and Adventures*, his semi-autobiographical novel *The Stark Munro Letters* and his published writings of the Southsea period, together with the local newspapers of the time; and it is a pleasure to be able to record here the unfailingly good-natured assistance I have received from the staffs of Mrs Sarah Quayle at the Portsmouth City Records Office and of Mr Alan King in the Local Studies Section of Portsmouth Central Library — especially the latter, who have met my many requests for heavy-weight bound volumes of the old papers with never a complaint. Sources of quotes are mostly indicated in the text; any unacknowledged quotes of Conan Doyle are taken from *Memories and Adventures*.

Among current publications I have found the following particularly useful:

Richard Lancelyn Green and John Michael Gibson, *A Bibliography of A. Conan Doyle* (Oxford University Press, 1983).

Alvin E.Rodin and Jack D.Key, *Medical Casebook of Doctor Arthur Conan Doyle* (Krieger Publishing Company Inc, Malabar, Florida 32950, USA, 1984).

Owen Dudley Edwards, *The Quest for Sherlock Holmes* (Mainstream Publishing Company (Edinburgh) Ltd, 1983).

Sir Arthur Conan Doyle, *The Uncollected Sherlock Holmes*, compiled by Richard Lancelyn Green (Penguin Books, 1983) — in particular Mr Green's own long introductory chapter.

The following papers, published by Portsmouth City Council, present an interesting and well-documented picture of middle-class Southsea in Victorian times:

R.C. Riley, *The Growth of Southsea as a Naval Satellite and Victorian Resort* (Portsmouth Paper No 16, July 1972).

R.C. Riley, *The Houses and Inhabitants of Thomas Ellis Owen's Southsea* (Portsmouth Paper No 32, March 1980).

I am grateful to Mr Bob Reynolds of Cosham, to Pastimes Collectors Shop, Portsmouth, and to the Executive Editor of *The News*, Portsmouth, for permission to use some of their photographs; and to Mr Richard Lancelyn Green and Mr Stanley Mackenzie for the photographs of Dr Conan Doyle. Also to the Honorary Editors of the Sherlock Holmes Journal (London) for permission to reproduce certain material which has previously appeared in the SHJ.

Finally I should like to record my appreciation of the encouragement I have received, directly or indirectly, from two individual Conan Doyle enthusiasts, Dr Alvin Rodin of Dayton, Ohio, and Mr Terry Little, of the Eldon Arms, Southsea.

Conan Doyle's short stories and photographic articles are currently available in the following collections:

The Conan Doyle Stories (Galley Press for W.H. Smith & Son, 1985).

The Unknown Conan Doyle: Uncollected Stories, edited and introduced by John Michael Gibson and Richard Lancelyn Green (Secker & Warburg, 1982).

The Unknown Conan Doyle: Essays in Photography, also edited and introduced by John Michael Gibson and Richard Lancelyn Green (Secker & Warburg, 1982).

His early and lesser-known novels, long out of print in this country, have recently been republished by the American firm of Gaslight Publications, Bloomington, Indiana. The titles include *The Stark Munro Letters, The Firm of Girdlestone, The Mystery of Cloomber, The Doings of Raffles Haw, The Parasite, Beyond The City,* and *The Tragedy of The Korosko.* Gaslight's British agent is The Out of Print Bookshop, 58 Wood Street, Liverpool L1 4AJ.

Southsea 1986.   **GSS.**

Contents

CHAPTER I

1882 — The New Boy

ONE FINE DAY towards the end of June in the year 1882 a young man stepped ashore from a coastal steamer at Clarence Pier, at the western end of Southsea Common. He was tall, broad-shouldered, with plump cheeks, a well-developed moustache, and a pair of sharp, bold eyes which hinted that although it was only a month after his twenty-third birthday he had already been around a bit and could look after himself nicely, thank you. He was dressed in comfortable tweeds, complete with waistcoat and stiff collar and tie despite the time of year. With him he had all his worldly possessions: a tin box containing his top-hat (every Victorian gentleman with any pretensions to professional respectability had to have a top-hat, and consequently a box to carry it in) and a leather trunk. It must have been a pretty heavy trunk,

Clarence Pier, Southsea. A view taken in the early 1900s showing at left, the jetty at which Dr Conan Doyle landed in June 1882. (Photo: "Pastimes", Portsmouth)

9

because not only did it contain his best suit, spare pair of boots (shoes were not commonly worn by men, being considered effeminate), linen and toilet things and a few essential books, but also a brass plate inscribed with his name and medical degree, and his photographic gear, comprising at least a large wooden box camera, separate lens, and a set of glass photographic plates. Young Doctor Conan Doyle had arrived to seek his fortune as a general practitioner in Portsmouth.

We can imagine that he stood at the pier entrance for a few moments gazing at the scene in front of him. The general layout of roads and buildings was much the same as it is now: the wide green expanse of the Common stretching away to his right; in front, the Jubilee and Southsea Terraces, the Wheelbarrow Inn at the entrance to Castle Road, the line of Western Parade terminating at the Grosvenor Hotel, and the large pile of the Queens Hotel at the far side of Osborne Road. There were some obvious differences, naturally. No funfair, no masses of parked cars, no queues of buses. Unmetalled roads, bare of today's bushy trees. People walked, or had themselves pushed in spindly-looking bath-chairs. Ladies wore dresses done close up to the neck, with skirts which trailed along the ground and anything up to half a dozen petticoats underneath; just occasionally a daring glimpse of bare forearm might be seen above a gloved wrist. Mens' clothes were uniformly drab. Everybody, but everybody, wore a hat of some description. Public transport was the horse tram, and since Clarence Pier was the terminus of the line from the Town station there would be a number of these waiting in line, and the usual horsey debris lying about. Clarence Pier, too, was a genuine pier running out into water and carrying a large circular bandstand. Immediately to his left, where there are now a few shops, was the wooden front of the Esplanade Hotel — so constructed in order that it could be quickly dismantled in case of the need to clear the arcs of fire from the defences. Beyond that, in place of the Crest Hotel, there was Victoria Barracks and its parade ground, for Portsmouth was a military as well as a naval town.

Dr Doyle came from an Irish Catholic family, had been born and brought up in Scotland, and was to become famous as a great Englishman, but all that was in the future. He had qualified at Edinburgh University Medical School the previous summer, but already he was not without experience of the practical side of a doctor's life. While still a student he had made a seven month voyage as ship's doctor on board an Arctic whaler — an experience he always looked back on with pleasure. After qualifying he had tried the sea again, with less satisfactory results; on a voyage to the west coast of Africa he had gone down badly with fever, and the ship had caught fire on the way back. He had also taken vacation jobs as assistant to busy practices in Sheffield and Birmingham, where his duties had involved him in long hours spent making up prescriptions (it was normal

Dr Doyle's first view of Southsea. The view shows Pier Road and a corner of Southsea Common very much as Dr Doyle would have seen them, except for the electrification of the tramlines which was begun in 1900. At the right is Southsea Terrace, where he stayed for a few weeks in the summer of 1896.

A horse tram waiting to pick up passengers outside the Esplanade Hotel. The driver needed his heavy clothing, for his was evidently very much an open-air job.   (Photo: "Pastimes", Portsmouth)

The tram terminus, looking south towards the entrance to Clarence Pier. On the right is the Esplanade Hotel. Both this and the pier entrance were destroyed in the war.

(Photo: "Pastimes", Portsmouth)

Southsea Common. A picture taken around the turn of the century, showing the Ladies Mile before it became an avenue of elm trees.

practice in this country, right up to the days of the National Health Service, for a doctor to dispense his own prescriptions; their sale formed a not inconsiderable proportion of his income). Then, in the spring of 1882, he had gone down to Plymouth in response to an urgent telegram for help from a former fellow-student, Dr George Budd, a forceful but highly eccentric character who was rapidly building up a large practice there by the highly unorthodox means of giving free consultations and then prescribing enormous doses of his medicines. A partnership had been promised but there had been disagreements over Budd's methods, his letter had been intercepted, and then Budd had accused him of letting the practice down. "Very well," Doyle had said, "If that's what you think, I'll be better off on my own". A day trip to Tavistock had convinced him that there was no opening there, so he had simply packed his bag, got on an Irish steamer, and got off again at Portsmouth, perhaps for no better reason than that it was the next port of call and that Portsmouth, being a naval and garrison town, might be not all that different from the Plymouth he had just left.

So here he was, on a bright Saturday afternoon in the middle of the holiday season, a complete stranger in a town he had never been to, with less than ten pounds in his pocket and faced with the urgent necessity of earning a living. Not only that; as the eldest son of a family of seven whose mother had had to make sacrifices to provide for his education, he felt strongly that he owed her something in return.

Well, his first move was clear enough. He must find a temporary base, some cheap place where he could spend a few days spying out the land and trying to get organised. Where? Ask a native, of course. Leaving his luggage at the pierhead he got on a tram and asked the conductor (they had conductors then, and obliging fellows, for the most part, they were) to put him off near a street where he could find some cheap lodgings.

Now there is no published record of exactly where or when Dr Doyle spent his first few days in Portsmouth, but a little detective work — of which the creator of Sherlock Holmes would surely approve — may enable us to get near it. Our evidence will come principally from the following sources:

(a) *Memories and Adventures*, Conan Doyle's autobiography published in 1924.

(b) *The Stark Munro Letters*, an earlier and in some ways much more revealing book which he wrote in 1895, only five years after leaving Southsea. It is cast in the form of sixteen letters from 'Dr Stark Munro' (i.e. Conan Doyle himself) to a fictitious friend in which he describes the beginnings of his medical career at 'Bradfield' (Plymouth) with 'Cullingworth' (Dr Budd) and at 'Birchespool' (Southsea), as well as his early spiritual (not spiritualist) development.

13

(c)   The local newspapers of the time: the *Evening News* (forerunner
        of the present *News*), the *Evening Mail*, and the weeklies — the
        Hampshire Telegraph, the *Hampshire Post* and the *Portsmouth Times*.

In the 1880s Southsea was still growing, partly as a residential
suburb outside the bounds of the old naval fortress, (the part of the
city still known as Old Portsmouth), and also as a rather genteel
watering-place for summer visitors of the middle and upper classes.
The main lodging-houses were to be found in Jubilee Terrace and
along the sea front, and in the streets of tall bay-fronted houses
running south from Kent Road: Nightingale, Shaftesbury, Ashburton
and Elphinstone Roads, Netley Terrace etc. Visitors of the better class
would stay in these or in the hotels, and indeed Service officers would
often put up their families in such places for months at a time. We
know that Dr Doyle did not find a lodging in any of these, for it was
the practice of the weekly papers to print lists naming all visitors and
their addresses throughout the season, and his name does not appear
in any of these. We must follow his tram a little farther.

At the top of King's Terrace the tramlines forked, one carrying
straight on to the railway station while the other turned left down
Alexandria Road (now Museum Road). At Cambridge Junction the
latter crossed another line running from the High Street to
Commercial Road. It is more than likely that the conductor put his
passenger off somewhere near here, and that he found a billet in one
of the little narrow streets of Old Portsmouth, such as Highbury Street
for example, where at No.4 Mrs Mary Diehl had apartments to let. We
know that it had to be within reasonable walking distance of Clarence
Pier, since after striking his bargain — the landlady first offered him
a room at thirteen shillings a week, and then took another look and
brought the price down to ten and six — Dr Doyle walked back to the
pier, claimed his luggage, and paid a porter eightpence to carry it back
for him (thereby saving fourpence on the cab fare).

The Stark Munro Letters tends to confirm this conclusion. The author
writes:

> "I live in the queer health-giving old city of the past... In the High
> Street you can see the long iron extinguishers upon the railings
> where the link-boys used to put out their torches... There are the
> very high kerb stones, too, so that Lady Teazle or Mrs Sneerwell
> could step out of her coach or sedan chair without soiling her
> dainty satin shoes."

This certainly has the sound of Old Portsmouth about it.

It was a fine evening, so having settled in the young doctor decided
to take a closer look at his new surroundings. Putting on his best coat
and topper, he set forth for a dignified stroll, and ended up by getting
into a fight! He walked down to the park, "which is the very centre of

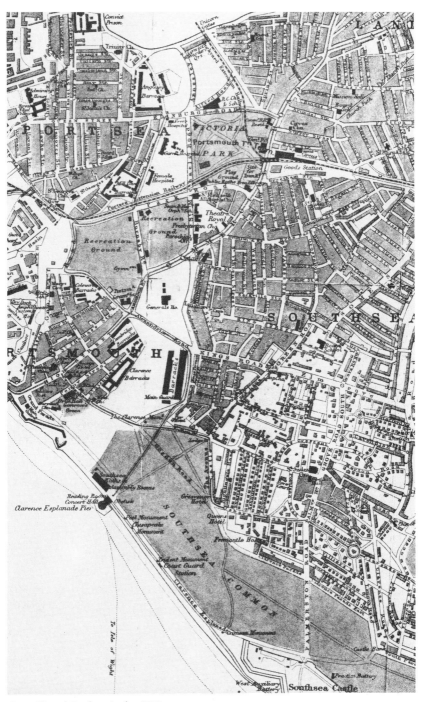

Street Plan of Southsea in the 1880s.

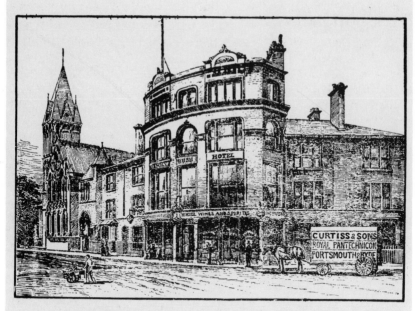

"BUSH HOTEL"

King's Road, Southsea.

COMMERCIAL AND FAMILY HOTEL.

WINES AND SPIRITS of the Choicest Kinds

*Bass & Allsopp's Ales,
On Draught and in Bottles.*

Proprietor - E. H. HILL.

The Largest Billiard Saloon in the Town.

Tables by Burroughs and Watts.

Head Quarters of the Cyclist's Touring Club.
SOUTHSEA.

An advertisement for the Bush Hotel in the 1880s. The sketch clearly shows the two small, flat-fronted houses, Nos 1 and 2 Bush Villas, squeezed in between the Hotel and the imposing pile of Elm Grove Baptist Church.

the place" (Victoria Park, that would be), sat and listened to the band for an hour, and was on the way back to his digs when he came across a small crowd of people standing around watching a roughly-dressed, half-drunken man in the act of beating up his wife. Dr Doyle was not the man to tolerate this sort of thing for a moment. Besides, he was rather proud of his own skill as a boxer. He sailed in, topper and all, much to the spectators' delight, and began swapping punches. Fortunately it didn't last long. One of his opponent's wild swings missed him and hit a sailor who, in Stark Munro's' words, "instantly took over the whole contract", so that Dr Doyle was able to escape, breathing hard but otherwise undamaged.

The Stark Munro Letters describes the scene of this encounter as:

> "a wide open space where several streets meet. In the centre of this stands a large lamp in the middle of a broad stone pedestal, a foot or so high, and ten or twelve across".

This is surely Cambridge Junction again, unless I am very much mistaken.

Having found his temporary base Dr Doyle now had to decide whereabouts to set up his practice. To buy a share in an exisiting one was out of the question; he would have to start his own from scratch. Being of an energetic and practical turn of mind he set about his problem in methodical fashion:

> "First of all I walked down to the post office and I brought a large shilling map of the town. Then back I came and pinned this out upon the lodging-house table. This done, I set to work to study it, and to arrange a series of walks by which I should pass through every street of the place... I used to have breakfast, get out about ten, walk till one, have a cheap luncheon (I can do well on threepence), walk till four, get back and note results. On my map I put a cross for every empty house and a circle for every doctor. So at the end of that time I had a complete chart of the whole place, and could see at a glance where there was a possible opening, and what opposition there was at each point."

We cannot say exactly how wide his search was, but he must surely have identified a clutch of doctors' surgeries around the Mile End area near the Royal Hospital, a few more along the terraces at the lower end of Commercial Road, and another bunch centred on the Kent Road area of Southsea. However, the outcome of his exercise is well known:

> "I found that there was one villa to let, which undoubtedly was far the most suitable for my purpose. In the first place it was fairly cheap — forty pounds, or fifty with taxes. The front looked well. It had no garden. It stood with the well-to-do quarter upon the one

side, and the poorer upon the other. Finally, it was almost at the intersection of four roads, one of which was a main artery of the town. Altogether, if I had ordered a house for my purpose I could hardly have got anything better".

This description of the situation of "1, Oakley Villas, Birchespool" in *The Stark Munro Letters* exactly fits that of No.1 Bush Villas, Elm Grove which Conan Doyle chose for his residence in Southsea. It was one of a pair of narrow, three-storey houses sandwiched between the large masses of the Bush Hotel and St Paul's Baptist Church, on the southside of the road close to the junction of Elm Grove, King's Road, Park Lane (now part of Castle Road) and Green Road. Even the fictional name he gave it, "Oakley Villas", is hardly a disguise, for Oakley Place was the name of a small area a few yards away on the opposite side of Elm Grove.

The Stark Munro Letters provides further confirmation, if such is needed, that "Oakley Villas" and Bush Villas were one and the same. On his first exploration of the empty house, the author entered a room in the basement where:

"in every corner piles of human jaws were grinning at me. . . But as I approached and picked up one of them the mystery vanished. They were of plaster-of-Paris, and were the leavings evidently of the dentist, who had been the last tenant".

King's Road in Conan Doyle's time, when it was one of Southsea's principle shopping streets.

The Census records for 1881 show that in the spring of that year the temporary occupant of 1 Bush Villas was indeed a Mr John E. Palmer, dentist, with his wife and three small children. One thing which Conan Doyle's writings do not tell us is whether Bush Villa had a bathroom. All but the very best houses did not, and had only an outside toilet in the backyard. There may have been a rudimentary hot water system, based on a back boiler heated by the coal fire in his living-room, but almost certainly Dr Doyle would take his morning wash and shave at his kitchen sink, using water from the kettle on his gas-ring.

The Bush Hotel, at the corner of Elm Grove and Castle Road (formerly called Park Lane), with Bush Villas in shadow. Dr Doyle enjoyed many a game of bowls on the green behind the Hotel.

All this area suffered badly in the great bombing raid of January 1941, and the Hotel, the Villas, and the Church (a fine big structure which had only been opened the year before Dr Doyle arrived) have all gone. In their place stand two low-rise blocks of Council flats. One, called Bush House, carries a plaque to mark the site of Conan Doyle's residence; it was placed there jointly by the City Council and the Sherlock Holmes Society of London on 17 November 1982, in the centenary year of his arrival. The other block is Oakley House.

Having found his house and fitted it out with a few secondhand pieces of furniture (not forgetting his doctor's red lamp · this colour has a different significance now), Dr Doyle was now faced with the real problem of starting his own business. A doctor, brand new to the town, must needs let people know he is there if he is to get any patients at all. He could put up his plate, but medical etiquette forbad him to advertise himself in any other way. Or could he? Never one to turn down a bright idea, he thought he had found one means. In the *Portsmouth Evening News* of Saturday, 1 July 1882, and repeated the following Monday and Tuesday, under the heading 'Miscellanous Wants', we find this discreet little notice:

"Dr Doyle begs to notify that he has removed to 1, Bush Villas, Elm Grove, next the Bush Hotel".

No 1 Bush Villas, Dr Conan Doyle's house, adjoining a corner of the Baptist Church. The house was later renumbered as 6, Elm Grove. Madame Lee opened her corsetry business here in 1903.

(Photo: courtesy of The News, Portsmouth).

King's Road in 1946, looking west from a point near the site of the Bush Hotel, and showing the road cleared up after the bombing and before reconstruction began.

(Photo: courtesy of The News, Portsmouth)

Bomb damage in Green Road, Southsea. This picture gives a vivid idea of the degree of devastation sustained in and around the area of Bush Villa.   (Photo: courtesy of The News, Portsmouth).

Clearing up in Elm Grove Baptist Church after an air raid. Only the shell of the building remains. The Church, the Bush Hotel and Bush Villas were all so badly damaged that complete demolition was necessary.
(Photo: courtesy of The News, Portsmouth).

King's Road today, looking east. Now a wide thoroughfare lined with blocks of flats, it was formerly a shopping centre. Bush House in the distance marks the point where King's Road becomes Elm Grove.

Removed? Well, who was to know that "removed" really meant "just arrived"? At sixpence per insertion and three for the price of two, this might well prove to be a shilling well invested!

It is this little notice which gives us our clue to the exact date of Dr Doyle's arrival in the town (his writings merely refer to it as June or July). If, as he says, it took him a week to find his house, then a week back from this notice takes us to Saturday, 24 June. Now among the advertisements in the *Hampshire Telegraph* at this time was one for the British and Irish Steam Packet Company, which operated a fleet of five ships trading between Dublin, Falmouth, Plymouth, Portsmouth and London. Single fare, steerage, from Plymouth to Portsmouth was six shillings. Sailings to London from Portsmouth took place on Tuesdays and Saturdays. A ship from Plymouth would reach Portsmouth on a Saturday, or just possibly the day before. So, Saturday, 24 June would fit... Elementary, wouldn't you agree?

It is not easy to say with any certainty whether Dr Doyle was being clever or just lucky in choosing Bush Villa as his base. He was certainly lucky in its situation. Elm Grove was at that time the northern boundary of fashionable Southsea, a compact square mile of tree-lined roads and walled gardens enclosing many of the large Italianate villas and elegant terraces which had been put up by the architect and developer Thomas Ellis Owen in the middle decades of the nineteenth century. Some of these properties were lost during the war, but a good many of them still remain to give an idea of Southsea's former spaciousness. Chamberlain's Directory of Portsmouth for 1881/82 lists the names of fourteen doctors already resident in this area. All of them lived in fine big houses far grander than Bush Villas, four of them in Kent Road alone, less than half a mile from Elm Grove. Dr Lestock H. Reid, of Bayfield House, for example, a comparatively young surgeon of 36, was able to support a household comprising his wife, three sons, three daughters and two nieces, plus a staff of cook, housemaid, lady's maid, and three nurses. Dr

The memorial plaque on Bush House, Elm Grove, Southsea. It was erected jointly by Portsmouth City Council and the Sherlock Holmes Society of London in November 1982 to mark the centenary year of Dr Conan Doyle's arrival in Southsea.

Nos 28 and 30, Kent Road, Southsea. This pair of houses, now a hotel, is typical of the standard of accommodation which professional men could expect to occupy in the 1880s. No 28, on the right was the home of a solicitor, and No 30 that of a doctor.

John Ward Cousins was another, whom Dr Doyle was to see a good deal of in the coming years. At 44 he was the senior surgeon at Portsmouth Royal Hospital, and he was also one of the founders and the permanent Honorary Secretary of the Portsmouth Literary and Scientific Society. Dr Cousins lived at Riversdale, a tall, heavy-looking brick house at the corner of Kent Road and Elphinstone Road. It is still to be seen there, with its old coach-house alongside.

Dr Doyle, for all his undoubted personal qualities, cannot seriously have expected that he would be able to build up a brand new practice by attracting patients from all these well-established men. Nor, of course, would he have dreamed of trying to. On the other hand, immediately to the north of Elm Grove lay a vast network of narrower

"Riversdale", Kent Road, Southsea. The former home of Dr John Ward Cousins, a friend and colleague of Dr Doyle. Dr Doyle must often have contrasted the size and prominence of houses like this with his own modest quarters in Bush Villa.

streets lined from end to end with plain-fronted terraced houses where dwelt the families of the many artisans and tradesmen who had been drawn into Portsmouth by the rapidly expanding work of the Dockyard. There was also the chequerboard of little streets with metallic names just to the south of King's Road — Gold Street, Copper Street, Silver Street and the others, once called Croxton Town, the very first part of Southsea to be created outside the fortifications of Old Portsmouth in the early 1800s. It was these areas, handily situated as they were only a few steps from his front door, which he must look to as his parish.

King's Road itself might have possibilities too. For whereas Elm Grove was residential, King's Road was then a busy shopping centre (curiously enough, these two streets have now reversed their roles, King's Road being lined with flats and Elm Grove with shops). Edward Hide, for example, Southsea's biggest draper, had three shops knocked into one, with a whole platoon of assistants to look after his bales of cloth and haberdashery (one of these, an unhappy young man called Herbert George Wells, was later, like Dr Doyle himself, to make his name in the world of literature). Any of these, or maybe some fainting lady customer, might suddenly need the services of a nearby doctor. Things were bound to be very slow at first, but given time and his confidence in his own abilities, Bush Villa might well become the seat of a respectable practice.

For a start, though, he would have to manage as best he could on the passing trade. It was slow going, but it did begin to build, in numbers if not in cash.

> "They have come in as well as could be expected. Some, like the little old maid who was the first, never returned. I fancy that a doctor who opened his own door forfeited their confidence. Others have become warm partisans. But, they have nearly all been very poor people, and when you consider how many one and sixpences are necessary in order to make up the fourteen pounds which I must find every quarter for rent, taxes, gas and water, you will understand that even with some success, I have still found it a hard matter to keep anything in the portmanteau which serves me as a larder."

One day, that first autumn, there was an accident near by, reported by the local paper as follows:

> "As the Marine Artillery were marching through King's Road a cab, driven by Mr Allen of Southsea, broke down. Mr Allen was thrown violently to the ground. On being picked up he was found to be unconscious, and was at once removed to the Hospital by a police constable."
>
> *(Evening News,* 31 October 1882).

Dr Doyle, as he sat in his empty front room reading of this dramatic event almost on his own doorstep, at once realised that he had missed the chance of a bit of useful publicity, and was determined not to lose out a second time. He did not have to wait long. A few days later there was another accident; not only did he rush out into the road to attend to the victim himself, he went down immediately afterwards to the Evening News office and personally gave them the item to insert. That same evening, under the heading 'Late Local News', there appeared the following:

> "Accident in Elm Grove. An accident, which might have led to serious consequences, occurred this afternoon in Elm Grove. As Mr Robinson, of Victoria Road, was riding in front of the Bush Hotel, his stirrup leather snapped and he was thrown to the ground, the animal rearing at the same time and falling partially upon him. He was conveyed into the house of Dr Conan Doyle, of Bush Villas, and that gentleman was able to pronounce that, though considerably shaken and bruised, there was no injury of any consequence."

Advertising? Not really. Just a little legitimate private enterprise, rather.

Dr Doyle liked the *Evening News*. Every afternoon he would walk along to Miss Gunning's little shop in King's Road to get his copy. At one brief period he was so hard up that he even gave up smoking — a real sacrifice for any Victorian gentleman, and with pipe tobacco at threepence an ounce — rather than go without his paper. At a halfpenny a copy the *Evening News* offered good value. Its four closely-printed sheets were packed with news of all kinds, local, national and international. Many of its advertisements carried names which still have a familiar ring about them. Mr W. Pink begged to notify that telephone communication had been established between his head stores at 110 and 112 Commercial Road and his Branch warehouses, so that his customers' orders could be fulfilled more easily. Elsewhere, less elegantly, a notice announced, all in capital letters, that TEA IS THE KING OF DRINKS AND W.PINKS IS THE KING OF TEAS. Alderman Pink, later Sir William, was the first of four generations of his family to combine running Portsmouth's biggest grocery empire with public service to the town and the nation. Messrs King and King were busy selling houses, as they are now; one in Stanley Street went for an even £200. Mr Timothy White had a chemist's shop in Elm Grove, and another in Commercial Road — though his name, like that of the Pink family, has been swallowed up by the supermarket chains.

To spend an hour looking through the back numbers of these newspapers is to transport oneself back through a century — only to realise that people themselves have not changed much. Fashions have altered and money values are different; we have different toys to play with but our aims and emotions are much the same. Men advertised money to lend, at unspecified rates of interest. Landladies extolled the attractions of their big houses:

"Bedroom and Sitting-room, well furnished, use of piano. Mrs Robson, Sapphire Villa, Albert Road."

It would be a colour TV now. Husbands published disclaimers for their wives' debts — though here is one with a happier note:

"I, James Meacher, beg to withdraw the statement by me relating to my wife."

There were some strange professions.

"Mrs Geo. Fulker, Ostrich Feather Dresser, begs to inform her customers that she has removed from 211 Lake Road to 40 Wycombe Road, Landport."

Whom did she dress, the feathers or their wearers? But there was evidently business to be had in feathers. At No. 80, Palmerston Road

Handley's Corner, Palmerston Road, Southsea. This picture shows Southsea's popular shopping centre much as it would have appeared in Conan Doyle's time. (Photo: "Pastimes", Portsmouth).

Handley's Corner after the bombing. Practically the whole street has been destroyed.
(Photo: courtesy of The News, Portsmouth).

27

(on the west side, where there is now a garage) Miss Lucretia Lait, doubtless aiming at a somewhat higher-class clientele than might be expected to be found in the neighbourhood of Wycombe Road, described herself as a "Milliner and Plumassier." Plumassier? I had to search my old Chambers for that one: "A worker in feathers; a feather-seller."

Teaching, notwithstanding the passing of the Education Act of 1870 which made universal education compulsory, was a profession still very much open to private enterprise. The *Portsmouth Times* and the *Hampshire Telegraph* regularly carried a column and a half of advertisements for private schools, nearly all of them in Southsea. As many as eighteen establishments for boys were listed in one issue, and five for girls — or rather, young ladies. Evidently, however, the competition was too much for one poor man. In the *Portsmouth Times* for Saturday, 3 February 1883 we read that "Mark Edwin Frost, of Trapezium Cottage, Kent Road, retired schoolmaster" — a Mathematics teacher, no doubt — "was adjudged a bankrupt on 30 January."

1883 was the year when one of Southsea's less successful enterprises was set afoot. On Saturday, 31 January notices appeared in the papers inviting applications for shares in The Southsea Railway Company, which was being formed:

> "for the purpose of making a short line of Railway from a New Station, at or near Fratton, to a central position (Granada Road) in the important and rapidly increasing watering-place of Southsea."

There were to be 5000 shares at £10 each, on which a dividend of four per cent was promised. The money was found and the railway was built, but it failed to survive the Great War. The station entrance, now part of a motor showroom, can be seen at the foot of Waverley Road. Not far away there is a street called Old Bridge Road, where there was once a bridge over this railway.

The Personal column, as Sherlock Holmes well knew, could always be relied upon to throw up an interesting quarry. Was there a hint of romance behind this notice, twice inserted?

> "The gentleman from Palmerston Road who accompanied a person to Mary Street on August 5th will oblige by writing — Miss Wilton, Post Office, Hill, So'ton."

Did he write? Did she remain a Miss? A romantic speculation, Watson, but destructive of the logical facility; we have insufficient data.

Life in the non-welfare state was distinctly rougher at the lower end of the scale. At the Portsmouth Police Court:

> "Sarah Wilkins, a Pauper, charged with refusing to work in the

workhouse, complained that she was placed in the Tramps' Cell, infested with rats which attacked her. She would have been worried had she not thrown things at them as they approached."

The magistrate (a man, of course), completely unmoved, gave her fourteen days regardless.

In the general news paragraphs accidents and calamities of all kinds abounded. "Terrible accident at Crewe"; "Awful disaster in America"; "Sad drowning case"; "Shocking attack on a Woman"; "Shocking case of Child Murder"... The Editor liked his adjectives, especially that last one. Some of the accidents were very odd indeed, involving animals as they so often did. Under the arresting, if somewhat inaccurate, heading "A Cannibal Donkey" in the *Evening News* for 21 September 1882 we read:

"A singular and horrible mischance occurred to a child... The lad pushed his head between the bars of a gate to look into a field, and then found that he could not withdraw it again. While fixed in this trap, a donkey grazing in the field came up and gnawed the boy's cheek until the bone was laid completely bare".

Well, whatever next. Violence and muggings are not new, either. On 4 January 1883, under the heading "Brutal Assault by Soldiers", there is an account of a police court case concerning a fracas at the Blue Anchor Inn, York Street, Westminster. Two soldiers had had a disagreement with the landlord and his wife, upon which the woman had thrown some water out of a quart bottle over one of them. Our brave lads weren't standing for that:

"The next phase of the transaction was that the husband and wife were found on the floor, bleeding profusely from cuts in the head inflicted by a soldier's belt and kicks... The man was unable to attend court, and his wife had a shocking black eye."

But wait. Whom do we see was watching the case on behalf of the police? None other than Chief Inspector SHERLOCK, B division! Did this name lodge somewhere in the back of Dr Doyle's mind, to re-emerge a year or two later when he was christening his most famous character?

There was no lack of nastiness on the international scene either. The following item, dated 9 January 1882, has an echo in innumerable films:

"George and Jim Fraley, the latter a mere boy, were arrested in the Commanche country, charged with stealing cotton. They were placed under guard at Hazell Dell. At midnight a mob, armed with shotguns, overpowered the guards, took the prisoners into the woods, and hanged them on the same branch".

It's hardly any surprise these days to learn that the town from which that cynical item originated was Dallas, Texas.

Chapter II

1883 - Has Made His Presence Felt

BY THE END of the year 1882, give or take a few weeks, Dr Doyle was probably able to feel that his practice, if not exactly flourishing, had at least made a lodgement in Southsea. Patients were trickling in, and although there may not have been any more happy accidents outside his window the winter weather would have brought its quota of coughs and colds; and, if some of these early patients could not afford more than one-and-sixpence for a consultation, there would be another shilling or so to collect for the expected bottle of medicine. "The garrison of Oakley Villas has passed the worst, and there is no talk of surrender", he wrote in *The Stark Munro Letters*.

His household had increased, too. Within less than a month of his moving in his mother had sent down his young brother Innes to be a companion for him — and possibly, who knows, to provide that little extra item of responsibility which might deter the doctor from undertaking any more wild adventures such as those he had got into with Dr Budd. Besides, it would effect a slight easement of her own household cares, something which the elder son had always been anxious to bring about. The arrangement worked well. Innes, a bright little boy of ten, fond of his big brother and delighted to be out of the way of his sisters, was thrilled by his new surroundings and enjoyed playing the role of the door-opener and general factotum at the surgery. Nor was his education neglected. He did not go to the Board School at Cottage Grove just across the way. Somehow the few pounds needed to send him to one of the many local private schools were found. Oakley House, Elm Grove, for example (Principals, the Misses Webber and Rider, assisted by Visiting Masters and Resident English and Foreign Governesses) charged forty guineas a year for boarders and nine guineas upwards for day pupils. Churchers College, Petersfield charged the same.

Oakley House, though obviously very handy, does not seem to have the right ring of masculinity about it to suit either Dr Doyle or his brother (all those governesses!). More appropriate candidates would be either the Diocesan Grammar School in Castle Road (Principal and Headmaster the Reverend G.H. de Fraine, LLB MRCP), or Hope House School in Green Road (Mr Edwd M. Bewlay, BA) where the young

Rudyard Kipling had been sent ten years earlier, while he was living with an aunt in Campbell Road. All these schools claimed to provide a Sound Classical, Mathematical and General Education, as well as to prepare pupils for entrance to the Royal Navy, Law, Medicine and Civil Service professions. Esplanade House offered Evening preparation for Competitive Examinations; it sounds suspiciously like a crammer. Whichever school it was, one hopes it did not follow too rigidly the traditional pattern of teaching as described by a former Headmaster of Portsmouth Grammar School:

> "Sit down. Study this subject with carefulness and industry. Make yourself thoroughly master of it. If you do not, you shall be soundly thrashed"!

One of Innes's teachers for a time was a Reverend E. Elliot, and in July 1930, shortly after Conan Doyle's death, he wrote a column of reminiscences for his own local paper. He was obviously much taken with the young doctor:

> "Few people that I have met have so impressed me by their personality and force of character. His burly frame, his genial smile, his manly bearing and light-hearted, optimistic way of laughing away all difficulties, as though he found life the jolliest adventure without a shadow or a risk — all these impressed me deeply. Their effect was heightened by a restraint and latent force which told of the strong man underneath this gay exterior — the virile character of one who was bound to get to the top of the ladder. I was not conscious of all this at the time and never dreamt that he would become famous. . ."
>
> (*Heywood Advertiser*, 11 July 1930).

Somewhat surprisingly the Rev. Elliot is much less definite about Dr Doyle's spiritual views:

> "His religious views were nebulous and vague; he would speak reverently of the Bible, but with a smile, as if he had no serious convictions. He was sceptical and tolerant but never antagonistic to religious faith. . ."

Dr Doyle did actually have very firm religious views, as we shall see shortly.

His household had also increased in one other respect. Feeling that there was a lot of wasted space in Bush Villa he had advertised his basement flat to let in exchange for services, and from a shoal of applicants, after one false start had been able to find an excellent housekeeper. In *The Stark Munro Letters* she is Miss Williams:

> "My treasure of a housekeeper. . . a tall, thin woman, with a grave face and an impressive manner. . . She is a marvel of discretion, and

the way in which she perjures her soul for the sake of the practice is a constant weight upon my conscience."

To the Rev. Elliot she was:

"A kindly old Scotchwoman who had been a servant to the family and was a mother to him and his little brother. . ."

She seems to have been an early exponent of the art of one-upmanship (a speciality in which Dr Doyle himself, like Sherlock Holmes, was no amateur), and took upon herself, in addition to her household duties, the job of receptionist. By making patients wait quite unnecessarily, or fixing appointments for them at highly specific times, she did her best to create the impression that the doctor was a famously busy man.

So now Dr Doyle had an element of Upstairs and Downstairs about his establishment, and could feel that he had his foot more or less firmly on the first step of the ladder towards professional status and prosperity. But he still had a very long way to go before he could aspire to the style of some of his neighbours. Mr George Lance, for example, a retired Judge of the Indian Civil Service, lived in baronial splendour only a few yards away at North Grove House, with his wife, four daughters, young son, a dependant widow, and a cook, parlourmaid, housemaid, nurse, lady's maid and a kitchen maid. At "Elmwood", a pleasantly commodious Thomas Owen house situated just off Elm Grove between Grove Road South and the Woodpath (on part of the site now occupied by Telephone House), with lawns and hedges on three sides, lived the Reverend Charles Russell Tompkins, a curate of St Jude's Church, Southsea. Not content with a wife and seven daughters to minister to his creature comforts, the Rev. Tompkins also maintained a cook, a housemaid and a nurse. It sounds as if St Jude's was a comfortable parish in 1883.

I suspect that the Rev. Tompkins was the original of the un-named "High Church Curate of St Joseph's" whose encounter with the new tenant of Oakley Villas is described in *The Stark Munro Letters*. The curate had been one of the first to call after the new doctor had put up his plate, with high hopes of welcoming him to the flock, and had been considerably taken aback when he was firmly told that the doctor had no intention of becoming a regular attender at his church or any other. For if there was one aspect of religion upon which Dr Doyle had formed firm views, notwithstanding what the Rev. Elliot may have said above, it was that of doctrine and dogma; and Dr Doyle, having once arrived at a firm opinion, was never the man to keep it to himself. The severe regime of the Jesuits at Stoneyhurst had served to toughen him mentally and physically, and had given him a sound grounding in English grammar, history and arithmetic, if little of the physical sciences; it had also served to turn him against all forms of sectarianism. He believed in a Christian God. He wanted, he needed to believe in the concept of a supreme Being who controlled the destiny of the Universe, but he could not share the blind faith of those who practised "the word" with narrow intolerance, or those who clothed it in pomp and Mumbo-jumbo. The extreme cruelty of the Catholics of the Spanish Inquisition and the fanaticism of Cromwell's Puritans had alike horrified him. Disdaining half-measures he had renounced Roman Catholicism for himself, even though it meant incurring the wrath of his family and losing the influence he might have had as the only Catholic doctor in Portsmouth. "I have no love for the cloth," he wrote:

> "Just as cotton, which is in itself the most harmless substance in the world becomes dangerous on being dipped into nitric acid, so the mildest of mortals is to be feared if he is once soaked in sectarian religion."

The "High Church Curate", or Rev. Tompkins if you prefer, received a barrage of these views and departed much offended.

Meanwhile Dr Doyle, having now established his beachhead, began to take what active steps he could to consolidate and expand it:

> "Above all, I learned a fact which I could whisper in the ear of every other man who starts, as I have done, a stranger among strangers. Do not think that the practice will come to you. You must go to it. You may sit upon your consulting-room chair until it breaks under you, but without purchase or partnership you will make little or no progress. The way to do it is to go out, to mix everywhere with men, to let them know you... It took some time to realise, but I speak now as one who knows."

Some of the first people he would call upon would be his professional colleagues:

> "It is the custom for a new-comer among medical men to call first upon the older, and the etiquette upon the subject is strict"

— and the first of these would be his near neighbour Dr Pike.

Dr William Royston Pike was a St Thomas's man who had obtained his MRCS back in 1872. He lived at Yarborough Villa, an elegant Owen house (now, alas, vanished) at the top of Yarborough Road, on the other side of the Baptist Church and less than a hundred yards from the front door of Bush Villa. He was an Honorary Surgeon to the Royal Portsmouth Hospital, medical referee for the General Assurance Company, an instructor for the Portsmouth branch of the St John Ambulance Brigade, and had at one time been Medical Officer of Health for Southsea. He also seems to have been a kindly sort of man and, far from regarding the newcomer as a threat to his own well-established practice, actually to have sent a few patients Dr Doyle's way. He had a young family of his own, and knew what the difficulties were.

In his spare time Dr Pike liked a game of bowls, and it may very well have been he who introduced Dr Doyle to the Southsea Bowling Club. Dr Doyle, being one of those lucky young men with a keen eye and good muscular coordination who can make a fair shot at any ball game, was later to become a familiar figure in much wider sporting circles, but it probably all began in those friendly matches with Dr Pike and others on Southsea bowling green. Another of the members was Mr George Barnden, who lived in Forbury Road, not far from the Town station. Mr Barnden was Superintendent of the Portsmouth branch of the Gresham Insurance Company, so we need not be surprised to find that before long Dr Doyle was appointed as the medical referee for this Company, thereby enabling him to enjoy one of those welcome little perquisities of the professional man through which, for an occasional few minutes' work, he might claim a fee of half a guinea rather than half a crown.

Conan Doyle provides an illustration of this kind of perks in a sporting reminiscence from *Memories and Adventures*:

> "I remember when I was a medical practitioner going down to examine a man's life for insurance in a little Sussex village. He was the gentleman farmer of the place, and a most sporting and jovial soul. It was a Saturday, and I enjoyed his hospitality that evening, staying over till Monday. After breakfast it chanced that several neighbours dropped in, one of whom, an athletic young farmer, was fond of the gloves. . ."

A friendly boxing match on the front lawn ensued, much to the enjoyment of spectators from the village. A weekend in the country, his train and cab fares to claim, plus a guinea at least from the insurance company as his professional fee — and all in return for perhaps ten minutes' simple routine work.

Every little helped: "A dentist over the road called Kirton sent me a few patients" (*Memories and Adventures*). This friendly neighbour was William Henry Kirton, LDS RCSI, who lived at Granada House, No.3 Elm Grove, on the opposite side to Bush Villa. Unlike doctors, dentists of that time were permitted to advertise themselves. Dr C.G.Knight, Surgeon Dentist, of 12 Queens Terrace, Kent Road (Consultations free, Pamphlets free by post) printed his name in large black letters around the margins of every single page of the advertisment section of the local Directory, and had a permanent little paragraph to himself at the head of the Local Intelligence column in all the weekly papers. We are not told whether any of his clientele found their way into Dr Doyle's surgery.

Dr Pike is one of the only two Portsmouth doctors to have been

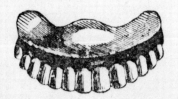

Mr. T. Good,

SURGEON DENTIST,

LION GATE ROAD,

LANDPORT.

The very best Artificial Teeth inserted over the most tender gums or stumps by the latest and most improved prinicples which, for natural appearance and comfort, cannot be surpassed; at half the usual charges.

SINGLE TOOTH FROM 5S.

A COMPLETE SET FROM 42S.

TEETH CAREFULLY STOPPED,

And, if necessary, extracted *painlessly* by means of

Nitrous Oxide Gas.

At Home DAILY from 10 till 7 o'clock.

Dentists, it seems, could freely advertise their services in Victorian times, though doctors of course were forbidden to use such publicity.

distinguished by a mention in any of Conan Doyle's memoirs (he is "Dr Porter" in *The Stark Munro Letters*). At some time in the spring of 1883, Doyle must have met Dr Weston. Dr Robert Ambrose Weston was about the same age; he had been educated at Manchester but qualified LRCP at Edinburgh in 1882, so they may possibly have met already in the Medical School. He was one of a number of doctors practising in the North End area of the town and had a house at Mile End, part of the old Commercial Road which has been swept away by motorway developments. What is more to the point here is that Dr Weston was a member of North End Cricket Club. There was quite a bit of cricket played in Portsmouth at this time, mainly between teams from the Services, and the match results were occasionally recorded in the weekly newspapers (so far as the *Evening News* was concerned, Sporting Intelligence usually meant only Racing); in a match between North End and the Unicorn Cricket Club, Dr Weston scored ten; in another against a team called OASIS (Old Alverstoke Scholars Improvement Society) he was the last man in ("Delayed at a case, Watson?") and made a duck. I have found no note of a score by Dr Doyle in any of the 1883 records, but it is evident that both doctors did play for the club on some occasions, for in October that year the *Portsmouth Times* published the following notice:

> "North End Cricket Club. This club, which it is proposed to re-name the Portsmouth Cricket Club, and of which the Mayor (W. Pink Esq) has consented to become the President, has issued the following averages for the past year:"

and among those figures there appear:

Batting	Matches	Innings	Times N/O	Highest	Total	Avge	Place
Dr Doyle	5	5	0	32	62	12.4	7th
Dr Weston	7	8	1	30n/o	75	9.3	13th
G.Hayter	8	10	1	10	21	2.1	22nd

Sherlockians will recognise the name of the less successful batsman, Hayter. In *The Adventure of the Reigate Squires*, Dr Watson relates how he and Holmes went down to Surrey for a short holiday with:

> "my old friend Colonel Hayter, who had come under my professional care in Afghanistan".

So, not only has Dr Doyle found another outlet for his physical energies, his social circle has suddenly widened rapidly to include the Mayor.

Another of his sporting neighbours with wide interests was Dr Charles Knott MRCS LRCP. He lived at "Lizville", Elm Grove (on the north side, just east of the junction with St Peters Grove) and had a practice at Mile End. Some ten or a dozen years senior to Dr Doyle, he was already a well known and widely respected figure in the town. He was a Surgeon-Major in the Volunteers (3rd Volunteer Battalion, the Hampshire Regiment), surgeon to the Ancient Order of Foresters, and held the appointment of Intendant General for Hampshire of the Masonic and Military Order of Knights of the Red Cross of Constantine and Appendant Order of the KHS and St John The Evangelist. He was Honorary Medical Officer to the Portsmouth Swimming Club, President of the Landport and Flathouse Rowing Club, and Vice-President of Southsea Tricycle Club. Dr Doyle became a famous tricyclist after he moved to London, but there is no evidence that he joined the Southsea club or even possessed a machine here; evidently he preferred at this stage to take his exercise in more vigorous forms, on foot.

Dr Knott later became Medical Superintendent of Portsea Island Infirmary (now St Mary's Hospital), and was founder and organiser of that hospital's highly reputed Nurses Training School.

Now it is time to mention Dr Doyle's other sideline. It is evident that though his practice was growing, if only slowly, it was far from being a full time occupation. There would often be hours in the day when his surgery was empty. He could fill many of them by reading, for he was a great reader, and often went so far as to make notes on what he was reading in an exercise book, to help crystallise his ideas, or because they might have come in useful later. But even this did not provide a sufficient outlet for his extrovert nature. The fact is, he was already becoming a bit of a writer. No, that is not quite the correct way to put it; he was nothing less than a compulsive writer.

Conan Doyle was a man possessed of an insatiable urge to communicate. Did he have an interesting experience to relate, an opinion to express or a philosophy to expound, he simply could not bear to keep it to himself. At one time or another he put every significant experience of his life into writing — some of them more times than once. He related his early medical experiences in *The Stark Munro Letters*; he retold them, in a shorter form, in *Memories and Adventures* thirty years later; and he used them again in *Round The Red Lamp*, his collection of medical short stories published in 1894. In one of these, *A False Start*, for example, Southsea appears as 'Sutton' and himself as 'Dr Horace Wilkinson.' Earlier, while acting as assistant to Dr Hoare in Birmingham, he began treating himself with the drug gelsemium (an alkaloid similar in its effects to nicotine), taking overlarge doses in an attempt to combat severe neuralgia. He noted down his observations, and communicated them in a letter to the *British Medical Journal*. At Plymouth during his time with Dr Budd he had attended a patient suffering from leukemia who had previously been a victim of malaria. He thought there might be a cause-and-effect relationship between the two diseases, and wrote to *The Lancet* to draw attention to this idea (and naturally, to himself). Already in 1883, before he had been in practice more than a year, the popular magazine *Good Words* published an article by him entitled *Life and Death in the Blood,* a piece described by the American medical historians Alvin E. Rodin and Jack D. Key as:

> "a tour de force, being not only superbly written but also at the very vanguard of medical knowledge, and even beyond in the uncanny accuracy of his predictions".

(These, and all of Conan Doyle's other medical writings, in fiction as well as non-fiction, are fully discussed in Rodin and Key's comprehensive *Medical Casebook of Dr Arthur Conan Doyle*).

He had already been writing on another topic. In his student days at Edinburgh he had become interested in photography, and had taken his clumsy box camera on holiday expeditions in Scotland and Ireland. He took it also on his West African trip, and over Dartmoor while at Plymouth. These were the days when photography was very much a do-it-yourself pastime; you made up your own emulsion, painted it on your glass plates before use, then developed and fixed them in your kitchen afterwards. Conan Doyle wrote up accounts of these excursions, and of his experiments with different processing methods, and submitted them to the *British Journal of Photography.* By the middle of 1883 no fewer than eight of them had been published (without fee, of course). These interesting pieces, forgotten for nearly a hundred years, were discovered by two enthusiastic English researchers, John Michael Gibson and Richard Lancelyn Green (authors also of the most comprehensive bibliography of Conan Doyle's writings), and republished in 1984 under the title *The Unknown Conan Doyle. Essays in Photography.* The style of the articles is chatty and occasionally flippant, very much in the manner of a young man writing letters home. They show how the future author was still finding his way towards a working narrative technique.

He wrote letters too, legions of them. He wrote to his mother almost every week of his life. He wrote to his sisters, to old school and University friends, to friends of the family, to his friend and former employer Dr Hoare. In a letter from Bush Villa, undated but evidently stemming from his early days there, he wrote, "The practice is stagnant. . . I want to get my name in the papers. . ." He knew he had it in him to become something more than just another anonymous general practitioner, but he wasn't yet sure what it was. Certainly he had no idea at this time that he would ever become a professional writer.

Besides all this, he had tried his hand at a bit of fiction as well. As a child he had sat at his mother's feet listening to her tales of ancient chivalry, of knightly deeds and their family history. As a boy at boarding school he had become the tale-teller himself, enjoying the role of romancer to an admiring circle of classmates. Why should he not try to capitalize on this facility, to put his stories into print thereby gaining a wider audience and the chance of a little extra money to boot? It was the era of the popular magazine, with weeklies and monthlies springing up almost by the dozen and editors competing with one another to find competent writers of fiction. Like many another would-be author he had his share of rejection slips or the occasional politely declining letter, but he had known the thrill of success as well. His first published story, *The Mystery of Sasassa Valley*, had appeared in *Chambers' Journal* for September 1879. It is an adventure story of diamond prospecting in South Africa with a little touch of ghostliness added, and it shows how even then he had not only the imagination to conceive an intriguing mystery but also the ability, through characterisation, dialogue and atmosphere to work it up to a span of four or five thousand words and carry the reader along to the solution on the last page. By the middle of 1883 he had had a dozen tales published, in magazines with names like *London Society, All the Year Round,* and *Bow Bells*. They brought in the very welcome sum of three or four guineas a time but their author was still denied the true satisfaction of seeing his name on the page, since, after the fashion of the time, they were all published anonymously.

One of these tales, *That Little Square Box*, which first appeared in the 1881 Christmas number of *London Society* and was later included in the collection headed *The Captain Of The Pole-star*, concerned the efforts of a passenger on a translantic liner to frustrate the actions of a couple of suspicious looking fellows whom he thought were carrying a bomb. It must have brought a reminiscent smile to the face of the author, sitting in his room at Bush Villa, when he read the following item in the *Hampshire Telegraph* of 16 May 1883:

"Infernal Machine on an Atlantic Steamer. As a steamer was about to sail on an emigrant trip from Liverpool, a box was given to a steward by a man who asked as a personal favour that it be conveyed to New York. After a day or two the steward became suspicious. The box was carefully opened by the Captain and others, and was found to contain a machine of such a nature that the Captain deemed it advisable to throw it overboard. The box was preserved and the address noted. Secrecy has been maintained at New York. The British Consul has been informed, and enquiries are proceeding."

A slightly earlier report in the same paper has an echo in another Doyle story:

"Dynamite Explosion at a Lecture. Whilst Mr Allen, borough

analyst, was lecturing at Firth College, Sheffield... on 'The Chemistry of Explosives', he made a number of experiments with nitro-glycerine. He placed a thimbleful of dynamite in a bucket of water, and applied to it a fuze. The explosion which ensued was so powerful that the bucket was smashed, and some of the people saturated with water and greatly frightened by the report. A portion of the audience left the building."

(*Hampshire Telegraph*, 2 May 1883).

Was it no more than coincidence that a story by A. Conan Doyle was to appear in the Christmas number of the *Boy's Own Paper* that year, entitled *An Exciting Christmas Eve, or My Lecture on Dynamite?*

Already in January 1883 his story *The Captain Of The Pole-Star*, published in the magazine *Temple Bar*, had brought him ten guineas, but he must have felt he had really hit the jackpot when in July the editor of the prestigious London monthly *The Cornhill* sent him twenty-nine guineas for *J. Habakuk Jephson's Statement*. Nearly a year's rent for Bush Villa in one go; over two hundred patients' worth! This story too was included subsequently in *The Captain Of The Pole-Star* collection. It is an excellently worked tale in which Conan Doyle presented his own solution of a '*Marie Celeste*' type mystery, where a ship is found drifting in the Atlantic with no crew on board and no particle of evidence on hand to indicate their fate. It was so convincingly written that one man at least, a British consular official at Gibraltar, felt it necessary to issue a formal statement that the story had no foundation in fact. Unfortunately for the author it still appeared anonymously. All the same, he must have got a lot of satisfaction from paying that cheque into his account at the Palmerston Road branch of the Capital and Counties Bank.

We have now arrived at the point where the medical, literary and social aspects of Dr Doyle's career in Portsmouth might be said to run together. Two colleagues whom he would have taken an early opportunity to call upon were Dr Ward Cousins, of Riversdale, Kent Road, who has already been mentioned, and Dr Claud C. Claremont. Dr Claremont's former house at 59 Green Road can no longer be seen, the road itself having been realigned in the postwar reconstruction so that it now meets Elm Grove some two hundred yards east of its former intersection opposite the Bush Hotel. In 1890, however, he moved to Petersleigh, a large yellow-brick property at the corner of Elm Grove and St Peter's Grove, just opposite Dr Knott's. This house is still there, though, like Dr Knott's, its ground floor front has been converted to commerical use. Dr Claremont was another relatively senior man, having taken his MRCS at London in 1877. Before coming to Portsmouth he had been House Physician at the Seamens' Hospital, Greenwich and an Assistant Medical Officer at Charing Cross

Hospital. He, like others, had a couple of Insurance Company appointments to back up his practice, and he was Medical Officer for out-patients at the Royal Hospital. Like Dr Cousins, he was an active member of the Literary and Scientific Society, and Dr Doyle's next step on his ladder of progress was to join this body. No doubt he felt that with that cheque from *The Cornhill* he could reasonably afford the annual subscription of one guinea.

In the autumn of 1883 this Society was entering on its fifteenth season. There was an earlier body, known as the Portsmouth and Portsea Philosophical Society, which was active during the second quarter of the century but which seems to have died out about 1860 when all its books and other assets (including a volume of 'Sherlock's Sermons') were sold off. Thomas Owen, the architect, had been a member. A deputation from this Society had had the honour of waiting on Sir Walter Scott while he was at Portsmouth prior to embarking for his last holiday in Italy. "We are but a Society of amateur philosophers," remarked the President, Mr J.W. Williams modestly, to which the Great Romancer made the Johnsonian reply:

> "Sir, amateurs are the encouragers and patrons of philosophers. They will be more distinguished as they are more encouraged, and will be rewarded by the greater diffusion of their opinions and discoveries."

The new body, at first called the Portsea Island Society for the Culture of Science and Literature but soon re-named the Portsmouth Literary and Scientific Society, had been formed at the beginning of 1869, and Dr Ward Cousins had been one of the original sub-committee of five convened to formulate its rules and constitution. A Council was elected, whose business would be to draw up a schedule of lectures to be given each season and to choose a President for the year. Meetings would take place every other Tuesday throughout the winter months, making eleven meetings in a season, beginning at 8 pm and ending about 9.30. The speaker would read his paper, there might be a question or two, then one of the regular members, detailed beforehand, would propose a vote of thanks and so the proceedings would be terminated. There would be no attempt to serve refreshments, but this was hardly a serious matter when everyone had a servant or two standing by at home to dish up a nice hot cup of cocoa, or glass of whisky, as the case might be.

The new Society flourished, and before long it seemed that most of the important professional men in the town (or at least, those with any intellectual pretensions) belonged to it — even if many of them had no intention of ever volunteering a paper. At the meeting of 19 November 1878, for example, when a Mr Arthur Byng read a paper on "Sea Serpents" , those present among the audience of 150 included

Lieutenant-General His Serene Highness Prince Edward of Saxe-Weimar (the Lieutenant Governor of Portsmouth), two other Generals, four Colonels, six Majors, eleven Captains, eight Reverends, sixteen civilian doctors, one Fleet Surgeon RN, four Surgeon-Majors, and various other Gentlemen RN (but curiously enough, no lawyers — or at least the local paper did not see to fit to name any).

This was the period, of course, when Queen Victoria's reign still had another twenty years to run; when men were men and women knew their place. A man would go through life, as my own grandfather did (he was born in the same year as Conan Doyle), without ever shaving his upper lip (that's why in those old photographs they all have those drooping walrus moustaches), while a lady might live without putting any colouring matter on hers. A certain amount of chauvinist piggery, therefore, was only to be expected. Ladies were not eligible to become members of the Literary and Scientific Society. They could attend the meetings, and often did in quite considerable numbers, but only as guests. This meant, however, that since they were only guests they were not allowed to speak; they could not raise questions or join in any discussion. One gets the feeling, reading the reports, that on the whole they found this sacrifice bearable.

The Editor of the *Hampshire Post*, no mean chauvinist himself, from time to time let himself go at the ladies' expense. "Bye the bye," he wrote in one editorial:

> "Cannot anything be done to stop the ladies from prosecuting their domestic employments at the Society's meetings? Several had the incredible vulgarity to labour at their worsted work while the President was speaking. The introduction of ladies is a very questionable scientific adjunct at the best; but they should be informed that needlework is as much out of place at a lecture as pipes and tobacco!"

The Minute Books of the Society are preserved in the Local History section of Portsmouth Central Library. The actual manuscript minutes are not very helpful, being nearly always written to a brief, one-page formula, but fortunately some thoughtful archivist has taken the trouble to paste in cuttings from the newspapers. These usually reported the meetings quite fully, with editorial comment as well, and it is these which make interesting reading.

On 7 December 1880, for example, a Mr W.B. Robinson spoke on "The Science of Teetotalism." He expounded at length on "The Evils Of Strong Drink" (all in capital letters, or so it must have sounded). "Strong drink is NOT a beverage," he thundered; "Teetotalism prolongs life!" Mr Robinson was the Chief Constructor of Portsmouth Dockyard, and one sincerely hopes that he had not been driven to these extreme views by the behaviour of Royal Navy personnel in his dockyard. Fortunately some redress was provided later in the meeting. Dr Miller (a very stout man), moving the vote of thanks, admitted that he himself always had his glass of whisky every day, and being quite sure there was no poison in it would continue to do so. He went on:

> "Men drank for the sake of conviviality and bonhomie, but the great mischief of drinking among women was the furtiveness of the habit."

(Here we go again, you see, ladies). Another doctor got up to second the vote. Dr Axford said that, with respect to taking alcohol day by day as a beverage, he cordially confessed that he did so, not as a stimulant, but because he liked it!

One is tempted to think that progess is a funny thing, sometimes. In those days tobacco was cheap and every self-respecting male smoked, but drink was considered a danger and there was a strong Temperance movement. Nowadays the pubs are full of young men, and girls too, but it is getting difficult to find a smoking compartment on a train.

Dr Axford had a practice in Clarence Parade, where no doubt he made a good living from ministering to the needs of the better-class visitors. He also, with Dr Cousins, had an interest in a private nursing home in Granada Road (First-class patients £1-1s-0d per week, second class 12/3d). On 31 January 1882 he read a paper himself entitled, "Food. What it is and How to use it" , which gave the Editor of the *Hampshire Post* another opportunity to exercise his wit:

> "Scientific Eating. . . It goes as a matter of course that the attendance was good. The ladies were very strongly represented. Perhaps they imagined that the lecture would have been accompanied by practical illustrations, and that savoury tidbits would have been handed around for their opinion. . ."

On 17 January that year Mr George Ollis gave a talk on Architecture (in which we find an early instance of the expression 'Jerry-building'), and which eventually resolved itself, as any topic connected with housing invariably did, into a discussion on the drains. The previous season he had spoken on "Healthy and Unhealthy Houses, or The Problems of Sanitation" — a meeting to which ladies, in deference to their delicate sensibilities, had not been invited. Nonetheless, the paper by Dr W.J. Sykes, the Medical Officer of Health, entitled "The Atmosphere" , which again concerned itself much with sanitation and sewerage, attracted a mixed audience of two hundred.

Also on to the scene at this time comes Major-General Alfred W. Drayson FRAS, another of those great Victorian figures, almost in the Doyle mould, who seems to have been able to combine an active and successful professional career with that of a prolific writer as well. He had served in India, South Africa and Canada as well as Great Britain, and had written several books of reminiscences. As a Captain he had been appointed Professor of Surveying and Astromony at the Royal Military Academy, Woolwich for a term of five years, and had done so well in the job that he was kept on for another ten. He wrote a book of reminiscences about that, too. He was the author of *Tales at the Outspan*, the *Manual of Military Surveying*, a book called *Common Sights in The Heavens*, and other more advanced astronomical works. One wonders whether Conan Doyle had the General in mind when describing the mathematical wizardry of the arch-criminal Professor Moriarty, though it is hardly correct to describe him, as one writer did, as "A specialist in asteroids". Besides all this, he was an expert billiards player. He had

No 20, Ashburton Road, Southsea, was the retirement home of Major-General A.W. Drayson. Dr Conan Doyle attended spiritualist seances in this house.

written a book on *The Art of Practical Whist*, numerous articles in *The Cornhill* magazine and *Chambers' Journal*, and some hundreds of articles (according to the *Hampshire Telegraph*, at least) in the *Boy's Own Paper* and *Every Boy's Magazine*. No doubt they were all fairly short, on practical themes like camping and scouting, and much concerned with the important virtues to young men of taking plenty of cold baths. One wonders whenever he found the time, and still more the energy, for all this mass of activity (perhaps he took plenty of cold baths himself). He was also, and had been for a number of years, a confirmed Spiritualist.

General Drayson had recently retired to Southsea. He first took up lodgings in Melville House, Osborne Road, and then moved into No. 20, Ashburton road, one of a tall, heavy-looking block on the west side. On 13 February 1883 he gave the first of several papers on an astronomical topic, and he was later elected President of the Society for the next year.

So, we come to the winter season 1883-84, and already at the opening meeting on 6 November we find Dr Doyle's name listed among those of six gentlemen nominated for membership. There is no evidence to show who it was who put his name forward, but it seems reasonable to suppose that it was one of the two doctors referred to above. Dr Claremont himself had read a paper to the Society in March.

General Drayson's Presidential address, entitled "An Hour in South Africa" , was popular in tone and well received. *The Hampshire Post*, with approval, described it as "Easy and conversational, free from the slightest suspicion of rhetorical clap-trap, and singularly well-formed. The audience seemed to see everything with the speaker's eyes."

At the next meeting on 20 November the six new members were duly declared elected. *The Hampshire Telegraph* now printed the name of Dr Conan Doyle correctly — it had been 'Canon Boyle' in their previous report, getting both his name and his profession wrong. The lecture was by a Surgeon-Major Evatt MD, of the Army Medical Department, on "The Army Doctor and His Work in War" — a topical enough choice, since the Afghan War was not long over and wars in the Sudan and South Africa were imminent. It was a talk which could have provided useful background material for the character of Sherlock Holmes's friend and chronicler, Dr Watson but we may doubt whether any such character had yet been conceived in Conan Doyle's fertile imagination.

On the evening of 4 December no fewer than 250 ladies and gentlemen, the second highest audience of the season, assembled at the Penny Street Lecture Hall to hear an address on "The Arctic Seas" by A. Conan Doyle Esq, MB CM. We might think that, facing such numbers, the new speaker would be every bit as nervous as he modestly claimed to be; on the contrary, he is far more likely to have been highly stimulated. With proper forethought, he had prepared his visual aids:

> "(The Lecture)... gave me a quite unmerited reputation as a sportsman, for I borrowed from a local taxidermist every bird and beast that he possessed which could conceivably find its way into the Arctic Circle. These I piled upon the lecture table, and the audience, concluding that I had shot them all, looked upon me with great respect. Next morning, they were back with the taxidermist once more."

> (*Memories and Adventures*).

The lecture was an unqualified success. The audience was enthralled by his evocative tales of the early explorers and his vivid description of the difficulties of Arctic travel. His conclusion in particular was received with great enthusiasm. The *Hampshire Post* wrote:

> "He advocated an annual Government expedition, to send a cruiser up every June so as to be ready to take advantage of a sudden break-up of the circumpolar ice, with the objective of securing the area for the Empire. Economists and utilitarians might argue as they would, but a glow of pride and joy would fill the hearts of the great Anglo-Saxon race when the day came for the British flag to be hoisted upon the northernmost pinnacle of the Earth! (Loud and prolonged applause)".

The President asked, as questioners will, whether it might not be a good idea to make use of a captive balloon to reconnoitre a track for the ship. Conan Doyle, still with a full head of steam up, said he thoroughly concurred; he believed that, did a man get blown across the North Pole in a balloon a ship could still pick him up in the seas beyond. Then suddenly, native caution prevailed. "He would, however," he concluded, "recommend such an explorer first to insure his life." (Laughter).

It was a fine high note on which to end his first eighteen months in Portsmouth, but what might have been a happy Christmas was marred by family news. First, his uncle Richard (Dickie Doyle, the cartoonist of *Punch*) had died on 11 December, but worse was the case of his father. Charles Doyle, an affectionate and talented but weak and somewhat unworldly man, had been "retired" from his job at the Edinburgh Office of Works at the early age of forty-six. Disappointment in his work, lack of promotion, and maybe mixing with the wrong sort of company had led him to overindulge a fondness for drink, and now alcoholism, perhaps complicated by the beginnings of epilepsy, had got such a grip on him that he was facing confinement in an institution. As it was, he had been gradually abdicating his responsiblities as head of the family, during Arthur's absence at least, in favour of the other man in the house. Dr Bryan Charles Waller, a consultant and University lecturer, had lodged with the Doyles for several years, and indeed had been helpful to Arthur during his training. Now Dr Waller was leaving Scotland to look after his family estate in West Yorkshire, and had offered the use of a cottage rent-free to Mrs Doyle and her youngest daughters. So the Edinburgh home was breaking up. Masongill, the seat of the Waller estate, was a tiny hamlet tucked away in a fold of the Pennines only a few miles from the little Westmorland town of Kirkby Lonsdale. It would mean financial security, yes. But at what cost?

Chapter III

1884 - Satisfactory Progress

IF THIS WERE Dr Conan Doyle's school report one might be tempted to put down "Satisfactory Progress" against the year 1884. His practice continued to increase. He got his name into the paper at least half a dozen times. He became prominent in another sporting field, and he made more new friends and colleagues, some of whose influence was to be more significant in the future than any of them realised at the time.

The Literary Society continued its season with six more meetings up to the end of March. William Kirton the dentist became a member, as also did the Reverend Henry Maxwell Egan Desmond MA FRGS, a clergyman of senior years who had taken up a comfortable retirement in St Vincent Lodge, one of Thomas Owen's detached houses in Kent Road. It is now in use by the Council as an old peoples' home, though part of its large and beautiful garden has been taken up by a brick extension not in keeping with the style of the original building. The Rev. Desmond, like others of Conan Doyle's Southsea acquaintances, gave his name to a character in one of the author's tales; in *The Hound of the Baskervilles*, written nearly twenty years later, we are told of James Desmond, an elderly clergyman in Westmorland, who might have been a distant heir to the Baskerville fortunes.

Dr Doyle, having already made his own major contribution, could sit back and relax at these other meetings, enjoying the nods of recognition and appreciation bestowed upon him by so many erstwhile strangers. He spoke up with a pointed comment or two at several of them, and indeed so impressed the elders of the Society with his interest and evident competence that at the Annual General Meeting on 29 April he found himself voted on to the Council.

On 12 February another large audience was addressed by General Drayson, for the second time that season, on "The Earth and Its Movements"; actually he was giving this one at short notice in the unavoidable absence of the original speaker, who was to have been Dr Nicholson, of Broadmoor Asylum, on the alluring subject of Criminal Insanity. General Drayson demonstrated, with the aid of diagrams and models, how the earth went round the sun, and the moon round the earth, and how the tilt of the earth's axis was responsible for the change in the seasons (O-level geography, we might call it now). He spent a lot of time going on about something called the Ecliptic, by which he meant the apparent path traced out in the sky by the sun over the year. We can take it as represented by the plane of the earth's orbit. Because of the earth's tilt, this plane makes an angle with the plane of the Equator. This angle, which varies very slightly over the years, measures about 23½ degrees; it marks the limits of the sun's travel north or south of the Equator, and defines the latitudes of the Tropics and the Polar circles. General Drayson referred to it as the Obliquity of the Ecliptic. His audience, we are told, followed him with earnest attention, if not exactly acclamation.

One who did docket some of the facts in his capacious memory was Dr Doyle. In *The Greek Interpreter*, which came out in the *Strand Magazine* for September 1893, we read how, after tea on a summer evening, Sherlock Holmes led the conversation between Watson and himself "from golf clubs to the causes of the change in the obliquity of the ecliptic".

He got another half dozen short stories published during the year. *Habakuk Jephson*, already paid for, came out in *The Cornhill* in January. The other five, with one exception, are comparative lightweights. *Crabbe's Practice*, in the Christmas number of the *Boy's Own Paper*, harks back to his days at Plymouth where one of Dr Budd's bright ideas for getting publicity was to fake a rescue of his assistant from drowning. The exception is *John Barrington Cowles*, a dark, depressive tale of a young man's obsession with a beautiful but heartless woman, literally a femme fatale, who ultimately drives him to his death. Several other of Conan Doyle's early stories — *The Captain Of The Pole-Star*, *The Man From Archangel*, *The Ring of Thoth* — dwell on this introverted and macabre theme of a man's hopeless passion which only becomes requited in death, and reveal an imaginative side of the author's character, a fascination with the horrific and the supernatural which is miles away from the outward picture of the genial, cricket-playing doctor.

Another *Hampshire Post* editorial is worth quoting. It arose out of the Society's meeting on 29 January, when Dr Bernard Guillebard in a paper on Life Histories advocated that every family (he meant every middle-class family) should keep a full record of its members' health and abilities, as well as their genealogy, in order to assist in finding suitable marriage partners and thereby improve the quality of the race (it sounds uncomfortably like Hitler's ideas of fifty years later). The Editor began with a reference to the many doctor speakers:

"We are always delighted to listen to the Doctors; they are invariably so interesting, so instructive, and as a rule so coldly and philosophically practical... the current session so far has been wholly monopolised by the faculty — "

and then went on to point out the practical difficulties of Dr Guillebard's scheme:

"Caste is an important factor in the marital equation. A lady cannot marry her groom with any propriety, however amply he may be gifted with physical and intellectual endowments. As we are fully aware, there are many foolish virgins in Southsea who would rather wither on the stalk than marry out of their circle..."

There must have been a good many of these unmarried daughters who privately fancied that life allied to the athletic young doctor of Bush Villa could be a fate a lot less worse than death, and who even attended the debates in the hope that they, rather than the chairman, might catch his eye, but there is no evidence that any of them succeeded. Not that he himself was any kind of a misogynist. Indeed, he went so far as to confess that on one occasion, at a dance, he ended the evening having proposed to practically every woman in sight. There had been a girl friend, with the unlikely name of Elmo, whom he had met on a holiday in Ireland. Another young woman, Jessie, is often referred to in his letters of the time. She was the daughter of Mrs Charlotte Drummond, a friend of the family in Edinburgh — but she seems rather to have been a chum of his sisters than of Conan Doyle himself. The truth is probably that at this stage he was so concerned with building up his practice and professional reputation as to make any thought of a serious liaison out of the question.

In the early spring of 1884, he was pleased to receive a visit from his sisters Annette and Lottie, with Jessie also, and he took them over to the Isle of Wight for a day. They crossed, as now, from Portsmouth to Ryde (but calling also at Clarence pier), in the two-funnelled steamer *Victoria*. We note, though, from his own account that:

"it was necessary for the Doctor to be back in Southsea by nightfall... the six o'clock boat was caught, and by seven the professional man was among his patients".

Not long afterwards there was another excursion. On Easter Monday, 14 April, a grand review of the Volunteers (what we should call now the Territorials) was held on Portsdown Hill. Some 16,000 part-time soldiers from all over Hampshire, including infantry, marines, artillery and cavalry took part in a mock battle followed by a march past (not an easy evolution to bring off on grass), with HSH Prince Edward of Saxe-Weimar taking the salute. One estimate reckoned that there must have been 100,000 spectators on the hill — most of whom got in the way at one time or another. The events were described in a full page of the *Hampshire Telegraph* of Saturday 19 April. It was a show which the townspeople had been anticipating for weeks past. Commercial Road shops and houses were decked out with triumphal arches, mottoes like "One Volunteer is worth Two Pressed Men", flags and bunting — though some local readers may be pleased to read that "Cosham surprised all beholders by the beauty and harmony of its decorations".

Dr Doyle went along with a party of friends — unfortunately not named, though young Innes, who was mad keen on soldiers, must have been one of them. They walked all the way from Southsea, four miles, in the morning but had had enough by the end of the afternoon and caught a horse-bus back, though grudging the inflated fare which the private companies had put on for the day. It sounds as if Conan Doyle might have been an early advocate for the muncipal ownership of local transport services. Naturally he carted his camera and stand along with him on both these outings, and wrote them up afterwards for the *British Journal of Photography*. His accounts duly appeared in the next two numbers, on 25 April and 23 May.

In March the readers of the local press were enlivened by a bout of religious controversy. The Reverend Henry Lindsay Young, Vicar of St John's, Portsea, already well known as a hard-line, no-fun-on-Sunday-or-any-other-day preacher, had chosen one Sunday to train his big guns on the local branch of the Young Mens' Christian Association, for daring to engage a Mrs Billington "who, he believed, was an actress", to give a dramatic recital in aid of funds for establishing a Portsmouth scholarship at the Royal College of Music. "A most heinous crime", he charged, "which rendered it undesirable for them to retain the word 'Christian' in the title of their Association". And so on.

The *Evening News* could not resist the challenge. Sparks flew from the Editor's pen next day. "A clerical firebrand", he labelled the Reverend:

> "A veritable Ishmael, his hand being raised against everybody presumptuous enough to hold opinions at variance with those he entertains. . . attacking Archdeacon Jacob, a venerable and learned divine, who is universally beloved for his consistent piety and his innumerable virtues, and launching vituperative thunderbolts in every conceivable direction. . ."

This produced its own response, and on Wednesday the paper printed three letters of increasing length and complexity supporting the Rev. Young's "eloquent and useful ministry", signed respectively "Veritas", "A.R", and "Yours humbly, A.C.".

These in turn led to the following eloquent, knowledgeable, good-natured and, you may think, eminently sane rejoinder:

> "Sir, I read with much interest the three letters which appeared in your paper of yesterday in defence of the action of the Reverend

St. John's Church, Portsea, burning after an air raid. Conan Doyle was an outspoken critic of the extremist views of the Vicar, Reverend H. Lindsay Young. (Photo: courtesy of The News, Portsmouth).

Lindsay Young, and was tempted to exclaim, with Shakespeare, as I perused each, 'Why, this is a more beautiful song than the other!'

The trio, taken together, would be of interest to the antiquarian. There is a mediaeval smack about them which wafts us back to the enlightened day when so-called Christianity took the stand against quoit-playing, the maypole, and plum-pudding upon Xmas day. What, because Mr Young is Vicar of St John's shall there be no more cakes and ale in the land? Think you that the mild man-god of Galilee looked stern when those children played whom he invited to come to him? "Worldly" is a word which the narrow-minded unimaginative bigot is only too ready to employ. The Roman pro-consul, steeped in the vices of the rising Empire, the lustful Sadducees, preaching temperance to the masses and living in luxury — these were the men to whom Christ applied the term. Who thinks now that He would mean it to apply to earnest and god-fearing young men, deriving intellectual and moral amusement from the lips of a lady who is above slander? As "Veritas" remarks, Mr Young probably cannot be shamed; and yet, unless his moral digestion is very strong, surely he cannot but feel some qualms when he thinks of the broad liberalism of our Saviour in the cornfield, and compares it with his own petty straw-splitting view of things around him? Is the designation of "Christian" to be withdrawn from a body of men because they listen to an account of how a child sacrifices its life in the hope of shedding a gleam of happiness upon the deathbed of a little mite younger than itself? This is the theme of "Billy's Rose", but of course Mr Young has not read it because it is (save the mark!) worldly and un-Christian. Thank God that there are not many who accept Mr Young's definition of Christianity, for if it held good, one would have to choose between Mohammedanism and Atheism".

The writer, who would be the last man on earth to hide under the cloak of anonymity, but who was nevertheless mindful of his professional position, signed himself "I remain, Sir, yours truly, ACD".

Conan Doyle felt compelled to rush into print a second time later in the year. On 15 September the *Evening News* printed a letter from a correspondent signing himself "Scire Facias" drawing attention to the existence in the United States of "several questionable institutions" whose practice was to grant so-called Diplomas by post to any applicant prepared to pay the fee of about 25 dollars. This produced a hurt and indignant response beginning "Sir, being the happy possessor of one of the above diplomas" and signed "William Edwards Wymond, MD Philadelphia and Associate of Arts of the University of Oxford". Others now joined in. "Spectator" queried the peculiar designation "Associate of Arts": "Of what Arts, prithee? Those of a sombre hue?" Finally, on the following Tuesday, came the unmistakeable voice of authority:

> "Sir, In ventilating the question of sham degrees and American diplomas you do the public a great service. In all other trades and professions an incompetent man is a mere inconvenience, of more harm to himself than others. It is different, however, in medicine. . . The so-called "University of Philadelphia". . . consisted of a small body of speculative parchment-mongers who did a roaring trade in worthless diplomas until the Government of the United States discountenanced them. . . There is a Medical Defence Association, which occasionally comes down upon these gentry and gibbets one to act as a scarecrow to the others. The public Press, however, is the best of all defences. I remain, Sir, sincerely yours, A. Conan Doyle".

With the summer weather came more cricket and bowls. At North End on Saturday 10 May Portsmouth Borough beat Southsea Rivals by 111 runs to 35, Dr Doyle hitting 14. On 21 May, in a close match against the Royal Artillery, the Borough won by six runs. Dr Doyle, promoted to opening bat, made 27 and 3; Dr Weston got 13 and a duck. On 10 June at the US ground they beat the Hampshire Regiment 94-79, Dr Doyle opening with 44 — almost half his team's total. Meanwhile, an account of the opening match of the season between two teams from the Southsea Bowling Club concluded as follows:

> "At the close members and friends adjourned to the adjoining hotel, the Bush, where a cold collation had been provided by Mr E. Hill (who is a member of the club) in his well-known style. Justice having been done to the good things, the company again resorted to the green, which in the cool of the evening was really most enjoyable, both to players and spectators. The amusement was kept up while the light remained, and the rest of the evening was spent in a convivial manner, under the presidencey of those popular members Drs Pike and Conan Doyle, the former gentleman favouring the company with a capital recitation from Tennyson. Some good songs by Messrs Clifford,Baker, Hill, Charpentier etc brought a most pleasant evening to a close".

The Bush Hotel also prided itself on its Billiard Room, "the most Commodious and best ventilated Saloon in the south of England". No doubt this is where Dr Doyle, who later added billiards to his other sporting accomplishments, got his early practice.

Mr Charpentier was the proprietor of a well-known printing and bookselling business in Portsmouth High Street, and publisher of an early series of illustrated Guides to the town. He too, like the Rev. Desmond, got a mention as a minor Sherlockian character. In *A Study In Scarlet*, the first of all the tales, Sub-Lieutenant Arthur Charpentier,

Royal Navy has a brush with the villain Enoch J. Drebber, on account of the latter's behaviour towards his sister Alice. The name "Pike" also makes an appearance; in *The Three Gables*, Langdale Pike is the name of a newspaper gossip columnist. I had always thought that this was a reference to the well-known Cumbrian mountains (though there is no record of Dr Doyle's ever having visited the Lake District), but the thought now occurs, was it a little joke on Dr Pike all the time?

Sherlockian enthusiasts are always on the lookout for coincidences of this sort. What do readers think of this one? At an inquest in Portsmouth on Elizabeth Sandford, a 16-year old barmaid found dead from congestion of the lungs, evidence was given by Mr William Henderson STARR, a London surgeon acting as locum for Dr LYSANDER Maybury, the police surgeon. In *The Three Garridebs*, Sherlock Holmes makes reference to an imaginary individual called Dr Lysander Starr. Too far-fetched? *The Three Garridebs*, a very late story, did not come out till forty years later. On the other hand, the villian in *The Engineer's Thumb*, a much earlier story, is Colonel Lysander Stark. There were two Dr Mayburys in the town. Both had been gold medallists in their training, and both had unusual Christian names. The senior brother, Aurelius Victor Maybury, had a practice at Mile End. Lysander, who was also the police surgeon, had his surgery in Hampshire Terrace, not far from Elm Grove.

In the general news reports the flow of accident reports continued undiminished, as also was the relish with which they were written up:

"Shocking Death. Mr Hugh Keen, a cab proprietor of Edinburgh Road, was in the act of yoking a horse to a vehicle when the animal ran away. Mr Keen, becoming entangled in the reins, was dragged along the road a great distance, his brains ultimately being dashed out by the kerbstone".

(*Evening News*, 16 September 1884).

Dr Doyle got another one to himself on 27 September:

"Accident in Southsea. About 12 o'clock on Monday, one of the employees of Mr Burton, St Paul's Square, was accidentally stabbed by one of his companions. The wound penetrated through the side, and narrowly escaped dividing the lung. The sufferer was conveyed to his house by Dr Conan Doyle, of Southsea, who dressed his wound, and he is now understood to be doing well".

Villains were afoot, some even in their own homes:

"Amy Stockham, the poor little girl whose father in a fit of frenzy placed her on a fire, has died of her injuries. Stockham will now be charged with murder".

(*Hampshire Telegraph*, 11 October 1884).

Condign punishment could be the consequence:

"The 'Cat'. A convict named Noon, who about three weeks since knocked down a warder in the prison at Portsmouth, and having taken his sword threatened to cut his head off, was on Monday flogged by order of the Director of Prisons. At the fifteenth lash his screams became so piteous that he was taken down for examination, but being found uninjured the flogging was resumed. After two dozen lashes had been inflicted further medical examination disclosed that it would be dangerous to his life to complete the sentence of three dozen. He was then taken down and replaced in his hammock".

(*Hampshire Telegraph*, 27 September 1884).

The following note records a peculiar and unpleasant perversion which had an echo in the Edalji case taken up by Conan Doyle in 1897, and even in Hampshire in 1984:

"Report of Maiming Horses in Ireland. Two valuable mares belonging to Mr Michael Nunan, Mallow, Kilmaconn, were found bleeding from punctured wounds, caused by a sharp instrument. No cause or motive has been found".

(*Evening News*, 17 September 1884).

Now, three more Southsea personalities who played important parts in Conan Doyle's life and career must be introduced. The name of H. Percy Boulnois appears frequently in the records of the Literary and Scientific Society in the 1880s. He was appointed Borough Engineer on 3 April 1884, and it is no surprise to learn that his first lecture to the Society, given on 9 December, was on "Portsmouth from a Sanitary Point of View". "Science in the Sewers", the *Hampshire Post* called it. He lived at "Ashenhurst", a square double-fronted house on the corner of Hereford Road and Albany Road, just off the eastern end of Elm Grove. His career in Portsmouth does not seem to have had a very auspicious beginning, for it was

"Ashenhurst", Hereford Road, Southsea. H. Percy Boulnois, a Literary Society colleague and personal friend of Conan Doyle, lived here during the period of his appointment as Borough Engineer, Portsmouth.

the subject of a Council meeting in early October. Members complained that despite the fact that he had been engaged at a higher salary (£600) than had ever been offered before, he had not only spent far too much time on duty away from the Borough but also had awarded himself no less than six weeks holiday; and they desired that the Mayor should reprimand him. The Mayor, solicitor Richard Marvin of Kent Road, said that he would convey a resolution but would not give Mr Boulnois a wigging. Mr Boulnois evidently survived this hazard, for he successfully took charge of a great new drainage scheme, wrote a standard textbook on Muncipal Engineering, and even got himself a rise in salary. He became a personal friend of Conan Doyle, and was a guest at his wedding to Jean Leckie in 1907.

Next, Dr Ford. We first come across his name in a report of a meeting held on 16 September to consider a proposal for the establishment of an Eye and Ear Infirmary in Portsmouth. He was selected, along with Dr Ward Cousins, to serve on a committee to work out the details. Arthur Vernon Ford MRCS, a son of the eminent solicitor and former Mayor Richard William Ford, was a few years senior to Dr Doyle. His address at this time was 14 High Street, but he later moved to Stamshaw and then to several addresses in Southsea. He was not active in sport or the Literary Society, but was a highly sociable type nevertheless, an Acting Surgeon in the Volunteers and Medical

The Blue Anchor Hotel, Kingston Cross, Portsmouth after its rebuild by the Portsmouth architect A.E. Cogswell in 1883. The inaugural meeting of Portsmouth Football Club, when "A.C. Smith" was selected as the team's first goalkeeper, was held here on 14 October, 1884.

(Photo: courtesy of Portsmouth City Records Office).

The Blue Anchor on the morning of 12 July, 1940, after receiving a direct hit the night before in the first air raid on Portsmouth. (Photo: courtesy of The News, Portsmouth).

Officer for the parish of Kingston. He became Dr Doyle's instructor in eye work.

Third, we come to a name which, ordinary enough in itself, has through the medium of Conan Doyle's pen achieved unwittingly enough, absolute immortality; for among those nominated for membership of the Literary and Scientific Society at the start of the winter season is none other than Dr Watson! This real-life personage was Dr James Watson MD. The fictional narrator of Sherlock Holmes's adventures is of course Dr John H. Watson. The name belonging to his middle initial H. is not specified; (Dr James had no middle initial). This Dr Watson was a Scotsman. Born in Edinburgh in 1840, he qualified at the Medical School and went on to take his MD while still a junior houseman at Edinburgh Royal Infirmary. There he was so highly thought of that he was shortly offered an appointment in the Foreign Service, and duly took up the post of Medical Officer at Britain's newest and remotest Consulate at the port of Newchwang, in southern Manchuria (its modern name is Ying K'ou or Yingkow). After eighteen years there he returned with his wife and two children to settle in Southsea, where he set up in practice at 70 Palmerston Road (on the west side, just about where the Chinese restaurant is now). Not surprisingly his first paper to the Society, read on 23 December, was on "China and Its People". Dr Doyle, as a member of the Council,

The Blue Anchor in 1985; single-storey only. and with a new front facade, but some of the old furnishings may still be seen inside.   (Photo: R.F. Reynolds, Cosham).

would have been one of the first to welcome him to the Society, and we shall meet him again in these pages.

As autumn approached and with it the end of the cricket season the thoughts of many sportsmen naturally turned to other outlets. Football was the obvious winter alternative, but "football" in the newpapers of the time usually meant Rugby. The Portsmouth Victorias, Portsmouth Antelopes, and Southsea Rivals were all rugger clubs; they played with fifteen men to a side and scored points by tries. At full back for the Victorias was a young man called A.E. Cogswell, who was later to become Portsmouth's best-known architect. His firm built schools, churches, the Palace cinema and other public buildings, but he is probably most remembered now for his many public houses; if you see a Brickwoods pub with its upper storeys done in elaborate half-timbering, such as the Borough Arms near the Guildhall or the Talbot in Goldsmith Avenue, the odds are that it was designed by Cogswell.

On the evening of Tuesday 14 October, however, a group of enthusiasts met in a room at the Blue Anchor, Kingston Cross and decided to form a club to play the game under Association rules. They would call themselves the Portsmouth Football Club. Chairman of the meeting, who also acted as Treasurer, was J. Lillywhite of the Portsmouth Cricket Club, and other members of that club were present with him. A field for practice, on the right-hand side of

Stubbington Lane, had been donated by Alderman G.E. Kent JP, the father of one of those present. R. Hemingsley, on the staff of the *Portsmouth Times*, was elected Honorary Secretary. A "uniform" was agreed on. The colours, appropriate enough for a Royal Navy town, were a foretaste of the strip of today's Pompey professionals: dark blue jersey with the Borough arms in white, dark blue stockings, white knickerbockers, and velvet quarter cap with peak. Secretaries of other soccer clubs would be invited to apply for fixtures.

Their first match was against Hayling Island, which they won easily by five goals to one. The next was on Boxing Day, again at home, against Cowes FC. The Portsmouth team was as follows:

Forwards:	J. MacDonald (Capt), C. Huddy, R.E. Jones, C. Gilham, P.J. Danver.
Half-backs:	R. Hemingsley, J. Dawe, J. Vincent.
Backs:	W. Adams, T. Huddy.
Goal:	A.C. Smith.

Consider that goalkeeper for a moment. The name Smith does not tell us anything, but is there not something familiar about those initials? Could they perhaps stand for Arthur Conan Smith? They undoubtedly did! Whether Dr Doyle felt that, whereas cricket was a gentleman's game in which he might very properly appear under his own name, the somewhat cloth-cap image of soccer might be off-putting to some of his lady patients, or whether it was just his own private little joke, we do not know. Whether he had ever played in goal before is highly doubtful; at Edinburgh he had been a rugby forward! But if a goalkeeper was needed, and that was the only way he could get into the side at first, he was certainly not going to be backward in coming forward, and if his professional standing demanded it, "A.C. Smith" he would be.

CHAPTER IV

1885 - A Variety of Interests

ON 11 FEBRUARY the Portsmouth Cricket Club held its annual meeting at the Albany Hotel, Commercial Road, but passed a resolution to make the Blue Anchor its headquarters in future. Drs Weston and Doyle, Messrs Hayter and Hemingsley were among those present; already the membership had risen to over 100. Their first season had been agreeably successful, with 28 matches won out of 34. Dr Weston, acting as financial secretary, reported income £23-8s-6d against expenditure £23-11s-3½d, but the deficiency was made up by a collection on the spot. Dr Conan Doyle was elected Captain for the coming season.

The new Football Club played its return match against Hayling, and won three-nil. They did less well away against Fareham, when A.C. Smith let in four — but Portsmouth had the excuse that they were playing three men short! Another name prominent in the early history of Portsmouth soccer appeared at this time. On 5 January a Mr Bernard Pares got up a scratch team to play against the North Lancs Regiment. He was one of four talented sons of John Pares, a local JP and a Governor of Portsmouth Grammar School. Bernard (later Professor Sir Bernard Pares, a well-known war correspondent and an expert on Russia) played at half-back; his brothers Basil and Lancelot were forwards. The eldest brother, the Reverend Norman Pares, also a great games player, had joined the staff of the Grammar School as assistant Classics master in 1881. He became a housemaster, living at Prescote, St Edward's Road, Southsea.

The Literary Society continued its fortnightly meetings. On 17 February Lieutenant-Colonel J.B. Richardson, RA gave a talk on "Our Modern Armaments". He praised the construction of the Spithead Forts, which ensured that "no fleet could approach, and bombardment of Portsmouth would be impossible" (Applause). On 31 March a long paper by Mr J. Charlton, Agent of the Chicago and Illinois Railroad, described a train journey from Chicago to Vancouver. The audience was much interested in his description of the luxurious American passenger trains, as well as his tales of the Mormon country and its people. Dr Conan Doyle again took notes, and we come across the Mormons in due course in his first Holmes novel, *A Study In Scarlet*, written the following year. From the floor he gave it as his opinion that Americans and Englishmen did not sufficiently understand one another, and that anything which tended to enable them to do so was of value — a sentiment which we might think just as appropriate today.

Other Societies met, for listening to lectures was a popular middle-class activity for the dark evenings. There was an Elm Grove Literary Society, based on the Baptist Church, but it did not include Dr Doyle in its membership. In February the Ratepayers Association met at the Red House Hotel, Church Road (off Fratton Road) to hear a talk by Mr T.B.Hayter (not the Hayter of the Cricket Club). His subject — guess what: "Portsmouth Sewage Outfall and Sewage Disposal".

Meanwhile, in the heat and dust of the Sudan, British soldiers were engaged in the campaign against the Dervishes of the Mahdi. The expedition to relieve General Gordon was too late, and Khartoum fell on 7 February. But the war, as wars do, had its advantages for some, as a paragraph in the *Hampshire Telegraph* of 31 January related:

> "Novel Way of Frustrating an Enemy. A Portsmouth firm (C. Mumby & Co.) is celebrated for the manufacture of aerated waters, and prodigious quantities of their famous drinks have been shipped to the Soudan. There the consumption is enormous; and after the invigorating contents have been drunk the bottles are broken into suitable pieces and placed on the ground outside the lines, much to the discomfort of any enemy marauders. Thus the barefooted followers of the Mahdi are compelled to dance back to their lairs, and regard these as the 'unkindest cuts of all'."

It was never like that in 1914, or 1940. The firm referred to was Charles Mumby & Company, of 34, The Hard, and their most widely advertised product (which no self-respecting serviceman of today would touch unless mixed with brandy in the form of a Horse's Neck) was Mumby's Ginger Ale, "A Stimulant Without Alcohol".

At Portsmouth Grammar School the Debating Society considered the motion "That this meeting would view with approbation the concession of the Franchise to women". It was soundly defeated by 40 votes to 26. The chairman of the Debating Society was a young mathematics student called Alfred H. Wood; in later life he became Conan Doyle's private secretary (Dr Doyle was against votes for women, too).

In the long dark evenings and the early mornings outside his surgery hours, Dr Doyle continued writing. Half a dozen more fantastic tales from him appeared in various magazines during the course of the year, as well as his last two articles for the *British Journal of Photography*, but he was still dissatisfied. If he was to establish any kind of a literary reputation he must at least get his name on the page, and that meant he must attempt something bigger; a full-length, hardback novel. He had already done one, called *The Narrative of John Smith*, but that had never even achieved a rejection; it was lost in the post, in transit to its first prospective publisher. On the whole he seems to have been relieved rather than sorry that this early effort never saw the light. But what a literary find that would be if even now it were to turn up in some dead-letter box — second only, one feels, to the discovery of Dr Watson's long-lost tin despatch-box containing his notes of Holmes's unpublished cases! So he had started on a second, called *The Firm Of Girdlestone & Co.*, a romantic adventure involving a kidnapped heroine, wicked businessmen, an Edinburgh graduate hero, and a whole Dickensian array of minor characters.

However, *The Firm Of Girdlestone & Co* was not going well. Too many interruptions, maybe. Also, he had something else on his mind: the practice. True, this had grown satisfactorily enough in the previous year, but, watching his accounts, he could see that the rate of growth was slowing down. In its first year he had made just £154. In the second, £250. It was climbing, slowly, towards £300. Now £300, or say £6 a week, was not at all a bad salary for a man in the 1880s, when an insurance collector might expect to make 24 shillings, and a shop assistant less than a £1, for a week of six fourteen-hour days. Even in the 1920s a builder's labourer could bring up a family on 35 shillings a week. On the other hand, £300 did not look very much when compared with what some of his friends and acquaintances were making. The Vicar of St Jude's for example, the Reverend J.S. Blake, got by on a living of £650. And £300 would never get him the big house, with its retinue of servants and his own horse and carriage, like the top people of Southsea had; or an organisation like Dr Hoare's of Birmingham:

> "a five-horse City practice, worth some £3000 a year collected from 3/6d visits and 1/6d bottles of medicine among the poorest classes of Aston".

An interesting sidelight on doctors' finances of the period is provided by a paragraph in the *Portsmouth Times* of 4 May 1887, when a Dr Charles F. Garrett was facing his examination in bankruptcy. He had come to Southsea from Gloucestershire in 1881, having sold his practice there for £600 and bought the business of a Dr MacIntosh for £1225. His first year's work brought in £600, but the load had been very heavy:

> "I had several large clubs left me, one had over 700 members, chiefly old men, who were always ill".

The club or panel was an arrangement, still common in the 1920s and 30s, whereby the members, usually working-class men, paid in a few pennies every week in return for "free" attendance by their doctor —

an elementary form of private medical insurance, in fact. Dr Garrett had been forced to employ an assistant (presumably unqualified) at £75 a year. He estimated his household and personal expenses at £400, but the real cause of his downfall was his sad admission "I had been losing money by racing for the last four years". Keen Sherlockians will not need to be reminded of the following piece of dialogue from *Shoscombe Old Place*:

> Holmes: "By the way, Watson, you know something of racing?"
> Watson: "I ought to. I pay for it with about half my wound pension".

So, bearing in mind the strength of the local competition, what could Dr Doyle do about it? A better degree might be the answer, perhaps as a first step towards specialisation. He decided to read for his MD.

The Edinburgh MD was a research degree; that is, you had to do some original work, write up your results as a thesis, submit this to the University and then attend in person at an interview where the senior members of the Faculty would question you minutely on all aspects of your findings to see how well your theories could stand up. Dr Doyle, unlike his colleagues Drs Pike and Claremont, for example, who were on the Honorary staff of the Royal Portsmouth Hospital, was not attached to any hospital or laboratory, so experimental work was out of the question. He must therefore do his research by thinking; choose some disease or complaint which was currently puzzling the profession, read it up in every textbook and learned journal he could lay hands on, marshal all the evidence as clearly and logically as he could, and see if he could construct a plan or strategy, previously untried, which might point the way towards a course of treatment. The disease he settled on — and it would be of great interest to know why — was Tabes Dorsalis, sometimes also known as Locomotor Ataxia: a wasting of the nervous system of the spinal column, thought then to be syphilitic in origin and an early stage in the progressive general decay resulting from that malignant and fatal infection. All through the winter he worked hard at it, sometimes having to travel away to consult the many authorities he needed.

Then both this work and his writing were overtaken by events of a much more immediate and personal nature. Early in March Dr Pike asked him to look at a patient of his and volunteer a second opinion. Jack Hawkins, a young man of 25, was living in lodgings with his widowed mother and sister Louise at No 2, Queens Gate, a large white-painted apartment building at the foot of Osborne Road, almost opposite the Queens Hotel. Their names had been included in the Visitors' List since the previous October. The young man was unfortunately subject to fits, which of late had been getting more

Queen's Gate, Osborne Road, Southsea. Miss Louise Hawkins, Dr Doyle's future wife, was a resident in this apartment block when her brother became a patient of his.

severe as well as more frequent. What did Dr Doyle think? The two doctors had no doubts about their diagnosis: cerebral meningitis, at that time incurable. All they could do was to minimise the patient's sufferings as much as possible before his inevitable death. Meanwhile, however, his fits were causing embarrassment as well as practical difficulties in the lodging house.

Dr Doyle then had an idea. There was plenty of spare space in Bush Villa. He would rig up a bed and a wash-stand in one of the top rooms, and they could move the young man in there. He and his housekeeper would be on the spot to look after him, and the mother and sister could visit him whenever they wished. And so it was arranged.

In passing, and purely by coincidence, we might note that the Visitors' List of that time included, as guests at "Homeleigh", Shaftesbury Road, a Mrs and Master SHERLOCK, from Ireland.

Poor Jack Hawkins did not last out the month. On Friday, 27 March, a sad little funeral procession left the door of Bush Villa and made its way, underneath the elms and along Albert Road to Highland Road Cemetery. In the one carriage behind the horse-drawn hearse sat the three mourners; the mother and sister all in black and with them, grim-faced in his shiny topper and best professional suit, the doctor under whose care the patient had breathed his last. It should be no surprise that something more than a mutual sympathy should grow between them. Louise, a pale, quiet, reserved but very feminine young woman, was far from unattractive. And if later, as the daylight hours lengthened, Dr Doyle's evening walks should trend more and more in the direction of Queens Gate, where Louise and her mother continued in residence, what could be more natural?

In due course they became engaged. Mrs Doyle, "The Ma'am", whom we may be sure had been kept fully in the picture throughout, came posting down from Yorkshire to size up her prospective daughter-in-law, not without a motherly qualm or two, no doubt. She needn't have worried. A modest, affectionate girl, not too young and flighty (Louise was a few months older than her fiance), who actually had a bit of money of her own (Louise had an income of £100 a year from her late father's estate), and who moreover was properly polite and respectful to her future mother-in-law — what could be more satisfactory than that? Just what he needs, she must have said to herself. It was soon agreed that the wedding should take place that summer.

Spurred on by this remarkable new development in his personal life, Dr Doyle soon put the finishing touches to his MD thesis and sent it off: one single handwritten copy only — at least he did not have to go to the expense of providing the three typed and bound copies that are demanded from today's students. It was entitled, with due poly-

Highland Road Cemetery, Southsea. The grave of John Hawkins, Dr Conan Doyle's patient and brother of his future wife Louise.

syllabic gravity, *An Essay upon the vasometer changes in tabes dorsalis and on the influence which is exerted by the sympathetic nervous system in that disease, being a thesis presented in the hope of obtaining a degree of the Doctorship of Medicine of the University of Edinburgh, by A.Conan Doyle, MB, CM.* In the course of it he had come to the conclusion that the disease arose as a result of minor veins of the back becoming constricted and cutting off the supply of blood to the spinal column, and had proposed treating the condition with nitroglycerine. Nitroglycerine? Yes indeed, a one per cent solution of this startling compound in alcohol was already in use at that time, under the name of Murrell's solution, as a dilating agent; it had given successful results in cases of angina, and there seemed no reason — if his deductions were correct — why it should not be tried with tabes.

Not all of Dr Doyle's findings have been confirmed by later work, but the examiners of the time were satisfied when they called him up to Edinburgh in July. As a wedding present to himself, he got a new name plate inscribed "A. Conan Doyle, MD".

Mrs Hawkins and Louise left Queens Gate in the middle of May and travelled north as guests of Mrs Doyle. For the wedding was to be held from Masongill, and the only account to be found in the Portsmouth

Masongill House, near Kirkby Lonsdale in Westmorland, formerly the family home of Dr Bryan Charles Waller, who resided for some years with the Doyle family in Edinburgh. Conan Doyle and Louise Hawkins were married from here on 6 August, 1885.

The Pennine moors near Masongill, West Yorkshire; the scene of Conan Doyle's story *The Surgeon of Gaster Fell*

papers is the formal announcement in the *Hampshire Telegraph* of 8
August 1885:

"DOYLE-HAWKINS. On the 6th inst, at Thornton-in-Lonsdale
Parish Church, by the Rev. S.R. Stable, Arthur Conan Doyle MD of
Bush Villas, Southsea, to Louise, youngest daughter of the late
Jeremiah Hawkins Esq, of Minsterworth, Gloucestershire".

Meanwhile, with the ladies and his other major pre-occupations out
of the way, Dr Doyle had time for some cricket; "A game," he wrote,
"which has on the whole given me more pleasure during my life than
any other branch of sport". The Portsmouth club had fixtures on most
weekends in June and July. He now appeared regularly as opening bat,
and if his scoring was somewhat erratic, including several ducks, he was
also featuring now as a fairly reliable stock bowler. The star bowler of
the side, however, was Robert Hemingsley, whose home was at 62
Chichester Road, North End. Messrs Hayter and Weston also appeared
frequently, as did a new recruit, Dr Keith Welsh, who was turning out
to be a sound middle-order batsman. In his late thirties at this time,
he was another product of Edinburgh University Medical School but
got his MRCS from London in 1872. He was Medical Officer for the
parish of Southsea and for the Portsea Island Union (the workhouse),
and was also President of the old-established Portsmouth Bicycling
Club. His home was in Bailey's
Road and he had a surgery at 77
Russell Street, Landport.

On Wednesday 5 August the
score sheet showed one startling
piece of information; a player
called Smith going in first made
21 and 22, and also took nine
wickets for very few runs. Surely
this could not be Dr Doyle in his
footballing disguise, the very day
before his wedding? Hardly; I
think we must assume that he
travelled up to Yorkshire on the
5th at the latest. A story he wrote
for the *Boy's Own Paper* the
following year called *Uncle
Jeremy's Household*, in which
Masongill is given the name
Dunklethwaite, describes the
journey: Portsmouth to Waterloo,
across London by cab, Euston to
Carnforth by the London &

St Oswald's Church, Thornton-in-Lonsdale,
Lancashire, where Conan Doyle and Louise
Hawkins were married.

North Western line, thence by branch line to Ingleton, and the last few miles by some form of horse-drawn transport. It would easily take a full day.

The mystery of the cricketing Smith is partially explained in the results of a match played against Sarisbury in the first week of September, when the names of both Smith and Doyle appear on the score sheet. Dr Doyle, celebrating his return from his honeymoon, made 40. The other was J.H. Smith, who knocked up the impressive score of 88. It is probable that he was the cricket professional at Portsmouth Grammar School, the "steady and civil Smith of Lancashire". He played in several matches for the Portsmouth club, and was also a member of the Victorias rugby team.

In the averages for the season Dr Doyle came in the middle of the order with an average of 8.8 from 13 innings. Dr Welsh had a creditable 7.3 from 5 innings. Hemingsley's bowling tally was 26 wickets for an average of 5.5 runs.

As late as 29 July Dr Doyle was still playing bowls at Southsea. In a return match against a strong side from Newport the club lost heavily, every member including Conan Doyle and George Barnden losing his individual bout. The green, now alas vanished along with the Bush itself, was most conveniently situated at the back of the hotel. At the conclusion, wrote the *Portsmouth Times*:

> "the visitors were hospitably entertained, host Hill catering in his usual excellent style. Dr A. Conan Doyle presided. . . With toasts and songs a very pleasant evening was passed".

It was probably a lot more fun than his lonely bachelor evening at Masongill on the 5th.

The Southsea Bowling Club was one of the first to take notice of its leading member's marriage. On 18 September the *Evening News* included the following item:

> "Presentation to a Southsea Doctor. At the Bush Hotel last evening a presentation was made of a handsome dinner service by the members of Southsea Bowling Club to their popular President, Dr Conan Doyle. Mr T. Reynolds (Vice-President). . . alluded to the recent marriage of their President, and wished him every happiness in his future career. The dinner service was a slight token of the esteem in which Conan Doyle was held by members, not only in his capacity as President but for his private character. . ."

The town itself was still striving to improve its attractions as a resort. On 1 July the Southsea Railway was opened with due ceremony in the presence of Lady Willis, wife of General Sir George Willis, GOC Southern District. Fifteen trains a day, including six with through coaches from London, was the intended schedule, but the line was too short and too slow ever to compete successfully with road traffic. Also at about this time a gentleman wrote to the *Hampshire Telegraph* suggesting that a stretch of the Common be levelled and graded so as to make it suitable for riding or walking upon. A Ladies' Mile, he would call it. Trees would enhance its appeal; elms, preferably.

Yet still the sordid side of life among poorer classes found plenty of space in the papers to send genteel shivers running through their more comfortable readers:

"A GIRL SENTENCED TO DEATH. At Durham Assizes on Saturday Sarah Dunn, a girl of seventeen, was indicted for the wilful murder of her illegitimate child, age 16 months, by placing it in a drain. The body was found buried and covered with mud, the search having been made at the instigation of prisoner's father. It was urged for the defence that the child, of which the prisoner appeared to be very fond, fell into the drain accidentally, and that the mother had hidden the body through fear. Sentence of death was passed in the usual form".

"Jos. Tucker, 37, shoe finisher, was charged at Nottingham Assizes on Monday with the murder of Elizabeth Williamson, 32, who had lived with the prisoner for nine years as his wife. Both were addicted to drink, and quarrels were frequent. Late on the night of 10 May prisoner returned home drunk. He kicked the woman and knocked her down. While she was on the floor he emptied the contents of a bottle of paraffin over her and then applied a lighted match to her dress. The woman was instantly in a blaze. Her screams attracted the neighbours, who extinguished the flames. The prisoner stood by with folded arms, and said 'Let the *** burn'. Five days later she died. Prisoner was found guilty and sentenced to be hanged".

Dr Doyle's newly married state did not hinder him much from continuing his career as a sportsman. On 17 October he and Dr Pike attended the annual dinner of the Crystal Palace Bowling Club at the pub of that name in Fratton. The Football Club had a couple of successful fixtures, A.C. Smith now playing at right back, but they lost 2-1 against Wimborne after extra time in the Hants and Dorset Cup. The team's performance, playing throughout in a pitiless downpour of rain against a side of many years' experience, was nevertheles good enough to attract a crowd of spectators and drew favourable comment from the *Portsmouth Times*. Norman Pares turned out for the club, and distinguished himself at left back in partnership with "Smith", and the teams were afterwards entertained to a meat tea at the Blue Anchor, hosted by Mr J.E. Buckle.

The Literary Society began its new season on 10 November under the Presidency of the Rev. Desmond, and with Dr James Watson one of the Vice-Presidents. The Rev. Desmond's opening address, a long, detailed and immensely learned discourse on "The Parsees" does not seem to have had the right kind of inspirational affect, for a fortnight later the audience numbers had tumbled from 250 to 60. On 8 December another Reverend, E.K. Kendall, a new curate at St Jude's, had only 40 listeners for his talk on "Pauperism. Poverty and what to do about it". In the discussion Dr Doyle gave voice to his own views, positive as ever, in which again we may detect a touch of modern socialism, and a hint of fascism as well!

> "If a person became poor, in spite of his endeavours to get on in the world, that person had a direct claim on the state... but professional tramps should be formed into regiments, and be compelled to work under Government in reclaiming the marsh land in various parts of the country. It would be better to improve the country by that means than to send them worthless to the Colonies".

To round off his labours for the year, he managed to complete *The Firm Of Girdlestone & Co* and send off the manuscript on the first of its travels. He would try the magazine publishers for a start; it should be suitable as a serial, then with luck hard-back publication might follow.

Did he spend Christmas in Southsea with his new family (Louise's mother was living at Bush Villa with them), or did they all go up to Mrs Mary Doyle at Masongill? The biographies are never clear on this, but for 1885 at least the answer is not in doubt; throughout the break A.C. Smith was playing regularly with the PFC.

CHAPTER V

1886 - Holmes and Watson

IT WAS A hard winter. In January there were gales all round the British coasts, and severe frosts. The West Highlands had their worst snowstorm in years, and snow fell in the Midlands, the south, and in Devon. With the Common blanketed in white, and the roads churned up into a smelly brown slush by the horse traffic, the ladies of Southsea had to hitch up their trailing skirts and cling to one another for support on their perilous expeditions to Mr Hide's or Mr Handley's in Palmerston Road.

The severe weather did not prevent the Portsmouth Football Club from carrying out a very successful first full season. In four matches between Christmas and New Year they scored 21 goals to only 4 against. On 30 December they beat a Royal Marines team 10-0, when:

> "the full backs, particularly A.C. Smith, did what work devolved upon them so satisfactorily that the office of the Portsmouth goalkeeper was quite a sinecure"

to quote the *Portsmouth Times*. "Heavy punting" was their correspondent's favourite epithet for the play of A.C. Smith. Indeed, at six feet two and fifteen stone, in the full vigour and confidence of his first year of married life, Dr Doyle must have presented a formidable sight to any opposing winger; a prudent man would keep well out of the way when "Smith" was shaping up for a clearance kick. Throughout February and March he turned out regularly at right back, with a succession of different partners: Pinfold, Peters, Hemingsley. By the end of the month the Club's tally read: played 22, won 15, drawn 3, lost 3, goals 80-28.

Bernard Pares's team, now calling themselves The Sunflowers, also made several appearances. The fourth brother, the Reverend Norman, who had a dual appointment as curate at St Jude's and Assistant Classical Master at the Grammar School, also turned out a couple of times, but for the Portsmouth Club and not his brother's side. On both occasions he played at back, and "Smith" reverted to his old place in goal; in a match against HMS Marlborough played in heavy weather on 20 March it was the "heavy punting of the borough goalkeeper" which deserved mention.

It would be interesting to know by what name Dr Doyle's own friends and teammates referred to him on the field, or in the pub afterwards. Obviously they were all in on the Smith joke with him, but we don't know to what lengths he wished to take it. "Pass, Smith!", or "Well played, Smith!" dosen't sound right, somehow. Men in the excitement of play or conviviality are not usually so formal with one another; Christian names, or often nicknames, are the norm. "Smithy" might do, certainly far better than "Smith", but "Arthur", I think, is unlikely. Victorians on the whole were not Christian name men; there was far too much class-consciousness for that, especially in varied company, and a doctor had to remember his position at all times. After all, Holmes and Watson were just that to one another, even after seventeen years of sharing the same apartment; only Holmes's brother Mycroft is ever seen to refer to him as Sherlock. Perhaps "Doctor" would be an acceptable way out; "Right, Doctor!" sounds quite well. Certainly not "Doc", though; I can't see Dr Doyle putting up readily with a twentieth-century abbreviation like "Doc", no matter how freely the after-match beer was circulating.

The lack of available playing fields during much of January had at least one advantage for Dr Doyle; it gave him time to prepare his next talk for the Literary Society. On the 19th he rose before an audience of 100 to speak on the subject of one of his literary heroes, the great Scottish historian and philosopher Thomas Carlyle; an author not much read now outside academic circles, a hard and deep but cynical and pessimistic thinker, whose attitude to life might be exemplified by one of his sayings: "A well-written life is almost as rare as a well-spent one". In a long paper Dr Doyle presented a comprehensive account of Carlyle's life and his major works. "His horror of cant and conventionality", he declared with approval, "caused him to be looked on as some strange wild animal", but unfortunately "the strange and obscure style in which he wrote prevented his works from reaching the lower classes. . ."

Despite his evident enthusiasm and his own great natural gift for words his talk on Carlyle seems to have been several degrees less of a sensation than his exciting account of life in the Arctic seas had been. No real discussion followed it; just polite applause, a brief vote of thanks and an even briefer reply. We get the impression that the great writer's works were just as unfamiliar to that audience (not one of whom, of course, would have dreamed of considering himself as belonging to Dr Doyle's lower classes) as they are to most of us today. All the newspapers reported the meeting, but the *Hampshire Post* took the trouble to print a long editorial as well. This editor at least was one who knew his Carlyle. He began by deploring the general lack of controversy and argument in the Society's proceedings:

"The President... evidently knew his audience, and never seemed to think that anything more than a general Amen was to be extorted from them".

He then criticised the conventional views of the speaker:

"Dr Doyle proved a stronger clansman than a medico, and rolled his eyes heavenwards throughout his discourse in a sort of holy frenzy... Why did he not mention the darker side of Carlyle's character — a bad and cruel schoolmaster, victim of a shocking digestion, who found his household economy more than he could manage, whose works were as barbarous in sentiment as in literary style — " etc.

Dr Doyle, who could be sensitive to criticism, stoutly defended himself in a long but good-natured and polite letter which the paper printed the following weekend. "What concerned me more particularly in writing this letter", he concluded:

"was the defence of his private character. As flies settle on the least sound portion of the meat, so critics love to dwell on the weaker side of a great mind".

Returning the compliment, the Editor stated that it was not normally his policy to print comments on his editorials, but that he did so exceptionally on this occasion because he felt that the Society had closed its own debate prematurely.

Dr Doyle certainly valued the Society for the experience and the many useful contacts it gave him, but he liked to preserve a cheerfully lightweight attitude to the lectures themselves (except, perhaps, his own). "I have many pleasant and some comic reminiscences of this Society", he wrote in *Memories and Adventures*.

"We kept the sacred flame burning in the old city with our weekly papers and discussions during the long winters... We had some weird people and incidents at these debates. I remember one very learned discussion on fossils and the age of the strata, which was ended by a cadaverous Major-General of the Evangelical persuasion who rose and said in a hollow voice that all this speculation was in vain, since we knew on an authority which could not possibly be questioned that the world was made exactly five thousand eight hundred and ninety years ago. This put the lid on the debate and we all crept home to bed".

Several senior Army officers besides General Drayson had chosen to retire to Southsea, and some of them lent their dignity and experience to the affairs of the Literary Society. Lieutenant-General Thomas N.Harward, a former Gunner, had rented Kingston House, one of a group of four handsome Georgian villas on the south side of Kingston

Crescent, next to the junction with Kingston Road. In a long career with the Indian Army he had served throughout the Mutiny and taken part in the relief of Lucknow. General John William Cox CB had an even more distinguished career. He was a veteran of the First Afghan War of 1840-42, having served with the 13th Light Infantry in Brigadier "Fighting Bob" Sale's force at Jellalabad. He had been at the siege of Sebastopol in the Crimean War and was mentioned in dispatches several times during his later service in India. He was a near neighbour of Dr Guillebard's on South Parade. It may well have been his conversations with these two members of the Society which influenced Dr Doyle in providing an Indian Army background to his first two Sherlock Holmes stories. In *A Study In Scarlet* Dr Watson has just returned from the Second Afghan War, and *The Sign Of Four* centres around a box of treasure stolen during the Indian Mutiny. At the same time, he did not forget his attachment to the great Scots thinker, and when later the fancy took him to endow Sherlock Holmes with a wide literary acquaintance, the name of Thomas Carlyle was one of those which he allowed to drop carelessly into the detective's conversation.

As in the previous season, the doctors continued to play a prominent part in the Society's affairs. On 2 February Dr Ward Cousins left his secretarial chair to present a talk entitled "Mental Aptitudes, with particular respect to Education and Selection of Occupation". He chose to speak extempore, or at least only from notes rather than a script, which led one correspondent of the *Hampshire Post* to complain that "if it be a mistake to limit the time, Dr Cousins certainly did not fall into that error". One suspects, indeed, that most if not all the Society's speakers, like any inexperienced lecturer, overestimated the amount of material they needed to fill in their time, and so allowed themselves to ramble on far beyond the audience's attention-span. On 16 February Dr Axford spoke on "Funeral Customs", making an early plea in favour of cremation in place of interment. Then it was the turn of the other professionals, the clergy. The Reverend W.M.Stern gave an account of the life and work of the German Jewish philosopher Moses Mendelssohn, described in the discussion by Dr Doyle as "one of the morning stars of German literature". (He was the grandfather of the composer). And the Reverend A. Halliday spoke on "The Science of Mind in relation to the Science of Morals", a piece described by the *Hampshire Post* as "so abstruse and complicated that the speaker lost his way as well as his audience".

Perhaps it was this last paper, or one very like it, which Conan Doyle had in mind in his short story *The Voice Of Science*, which appeared in an early number of the *Strand Magazine* in 1891, in which he poked gentle fun at these literary and scientific gatherings. The scene is again

Birchespool, his fictional name for Southsea, but he transfers the action to The Lindens, the commodious villa of Mrs Esdaile:

> "a lady of quite remarkable scientific attainments. As honorary secretary of the ladies branch of the local Eclectic Society, she shone with a never-failing brilliance. It was even whispered that on the occasion of the delivery of Professor Tomlinson's suggestive lecture 'On the Perigenesis of the Plastidule' she was the only woman in the room who could follow the lecturer even as far as the end of his title".

Was there a hint of envy, or merely ambition, in the following sentence, written at a time when his practice was still only making £300 a year?

> "It would have been a strange thing had Mrs Esdaile not been popular among local scientists, for her pretty house, her charming grounds, and all the hospitality which an income of two thousand a year will admit of, were always at their command".

Tongue in cheek or not, his own activities for the Society were so well thought of that in October of that year, at the instigation of Dr Cousins, he was appointed joint Secretary.

Already, much earlier in the year, yet another project was engaging his attention. He had decided to write a detective story. He was a great admirer of Edgar Allan Poe, one of the earliest writers of crime stories, and of the Frenchman Emile Gaboriau, but was critical of most of their popular imitators, whose detectives, he considered, relied too much on coincidence, or cheated by suddenly revealing last-minute clues which had been withheld from the reader. He wanted to create:

> "a scientific detective, who solved cases on his own merits and not through the folly of the criminal".

He already had a model to work on: Dr Joseph Bell, a gifted teacher and practitioner of the Edinburgh Medical School, whose assistant he had been while a student. Dr Bell's powers of observation and sharpness of deduction were such that he would often diagnose not only a patient's complaint but also his occupation and background from a few pointed questions. It is easy to see the origin of Holmes's famous "methods" in this story taken from *The Lancet* of 1 August, 1956:

> "A woman with a small child was shown in. Joe Bell said good morning to her and she said good morning in reply.
> 'What sort of a crossing did ye have fra' Burntisland?'
> 'It was guid'.
> 'And had ye a guid walk up Inverleith Row?'
> 'Yes'.

'And what did ye do with th'other wain?'

'I left him with my sister in Leith'.

'And would ye still be working at the linoleum factory?'

'Yes, I am'.

'You see, gentleman, when she said good morning to me I noticed her Fife accent, and, as you know, the nearest town in Fife is Burntisland. You noticed the red clay on the edges of the soles of her shoes, and the only such clay within twenty miles of Edinburgh is in the Botanical Gardens. Inverleith Row borders the gardens and is her nearest way here from Leith. You observed that the coat she carried over her arm is too big for the child who is with her, and therefore she set out from home with two children. Finally she has a dermatitis on the fingers of the right hand which is peculiar to workers in the linoleum factory at Burntisland".

Thus we find that Sherlock Holmes's opening words when he is first introduced to Dr Watson in the chemical laboratory of St Bartholemew's Hospital are:

"How are you? You have been in Afghanistan, I perceive".

American Sherlockian Societies, of which there are nigh on a hundred, like to take their titles from names of incidents in the canon; one flourishing one is The Afghanistan Perceivers, of Tulsa, Oklahoma.

Watson of course is duly astonished at this observation from a complete stranger. The explanation comes later:

"Here is a gentleman of a medical type, but with the air of a military man. Clearly an army doctor, then. He has just come from the tropics, for his face is dark, and that is not the natural tint of his skin, for his wrists are fair. He has undergone hardship and sickness, as his haggard face says clearly. His left arm has been injured. He holds it in a stiff and unnatural manner. Where in the tropics could an English army doctor have seen much hardship and got his arm wounded? Clearly in Afghanistan".

Conan Doyle knew that this facility alone would not provide a full character for his super-sleuth. He therefore endowed him with unusual physical strength and exceptional prowess in manly single-combat sports — boxing, fencing, singlestick; with the ability to disguise himself so completely in appearance, voice and mannerisms as to deceive even his closest friend and companion; and with expertise in various way-out interests, notably chemical research and violin playing (two skills in which he was notably deficient himself). His hero must also be a bachelor, to be able to follow an unconventional mode of life, unencumbered by domestic ties. A small private income would help, too, say £400 a year or so, just about what the author and his wife had between them. One other factor was needed, and perhaps here we come upon the real secret of the abiding endurance of these tales, which have never been out of print since they were first published — the Holmes-Watson partnership. Conan Doyle always liked to write his short stories in the first person, to give the extra realism of a narrator who was actually present at the events described, so he felt from the start that he needed a narrator for his detective. "He could not tell his own exploits," he wrote:

> "so he must have a commonplace comrade as a foil — an educated man of action who could both join in the exploits and narrate them. A drab, quiet name for this unostentatious man. Watson would do".

A professional man, not too brilliant an intellect of course — why not a doctor, whose medical knowledge could often be useful. And if, in that description "an educated man of action" we should see something of Dr Doyle himself, who is to say we are wrong?

Having got his characters, Dr Doyle mulled over his notes for a few weeks until he had his plot clear in his mind. Then, shutting his ears perhaps to the occasional sounds of the spectators around the bowling green at the back of his house, he sat down in the little upstairs room which Louise and her mother had rigged out for him as a study, and wrote the whole book in the space of a couple of months, March and April.

He had several changes of mind on the way. The title, at first *A Tangled Skein*, became *A Study In Scarlet*. The detective, called Holmes we suppose after the American essayist Oliver Wendell Holmes, was originally christened Sherrinford but at some stage was changed to Sherlock. And the narrator, who started out with the unlikely handle of Ormond Sacker, was duly transmuted into the much loved, much put-upon, Dr John H. Watson. Many bottles of ink and yards of paper have been consumed in the efforts of commentators to discover by what means Conan Doyle arrived at these two happy choices, Sherlock and Watson — whether he derived them from particular individuals of his acquaintance, or whether they just came to him out of the blue. The story, attributed to Dr Doyle himself, that he once scored twenty runs in a cricket match against a bowler called Sherlock, must be discounted, for the bowler's name was Shacklock, and in any case the match took place in 1890, four years after *A Study In Scarlet* was written! There was a Patrick Sherlock who was a fellow-pupil of Doyle's at Stoneyhurst, but that is not evidence enough in itself. Sherlock was a common Irish name, and the Doyles were an Irish family. We have already come across the name in three different contexts in these pages. As Holmes would say, we have insufficient data.

The case of Watson is, at first sight anyway, a bit more obvious. Surely

Study in Scarlet

Ormond Sacker - ~~from Soudan~~ - from Afghanistan
        Lived at 221 B Upper Baker Street
with

) Sherrinford Holmes -

        The Laws of Evidence

    Reserved -
Sleepy eyed young man - philosopher - Collector of rare Violins
An Amati -   Chemical laboratory

        I have four hundred a year -

I am a Consulting detective -

What rot this is " I cried - throwing the volume
: petulantly aside " I must say that I have no
patience with people who build up fine theories in their
own armchairs which can never be reduced to
practice -
            Lecoq was a bungler -
    Dupin was better. Dupin was decidedly smart —
His trick of following a train of thought was more
sensational than clever   but still he had analytical genius.

Facsimile of a page of Conan Doyle's notes for his first Sherlock Holmes story, *A Study in Scarlet* written in 1886.

he was named after Dr Doyle's colleague in the Literary Society, with a change of Christian name from James to John? (especially since in one of the tales, *The Man With The Twisted Lip*, Watson's wife appears to address him as James instead of John). Well, maybe. We have already seen how Dr Doyle would occasionally use the name of a friend for a minor character in a story, and whereas Watson is far from a minor character, it needs to be remembered that the author had no idea at the time that *A Study In Scarlet* was anything more than a one-off, and not the first of a long series. But Watson was a very common name among Scottish doctors. Sir Patrick Heron Watson was a leading Edinburgh surgeon in Conan Doyle's time. There was even another James Watson serving in China when the Southsea James was there. Again, you pays your money...

One very little known contender in the field that we can mention here is Dr Weston, Conan Doyle's cricketing friend. There is a school of thought among certain senior citizens of Portsmouth, some of whom can still remember Dr Weston attending their families, that Weston was the original of Doyle's Watson. Dr Weston himself, who continued to practise in Portsmouth up until his death in 1928, seems to have been the instigator of this interesting idea. "Did you know I was the original of Dr Watson?" he would say to his patients. In appearance he is said to have been rather short and slight, which is unlike the thickset, rugger-playing Watson. His favourite catchphrase, apart from the above, was "I've got a motto, always merry and bright" — a song from the musical show *The Arcadians*, which again does not immediately call to mind the stalwart scribe of Baker Street. In my opinion at least, Dr Weston's case must remain not proven.

So, the manuscript of *A Study In Scarlet*, the first tale to launch the characters of Holmes and Watson on an unsuspecting world, was parcelled up and sent off to follow *The Firm Of Girdlestone & Co* on its round of the publishers, by its optimistic but equally unsuspecting author. In it we are introduced not only to the two friends, with a little bit about Watson's background but nothing at all of Holmes's, but also to their comfortable lodgings at 221B Baker Street and their indulgent landlady (Mrs Turner in this story, but Mrs Hudson in all the others), and to the two Scotland Yarders, Inspectors Lestrade and Gregson "the pick of a bad lot" — although in fact they were only the first of a dozen or so police officers of varying ability who were to be encountered later. We also meet the Baker Street Irregulars, the bunch of street urchins whom Holmes uses as his eyes and ears, and who have given their name to the oldest and most distinguished of American Societies, the Baker Street Irregulars of New York. We see Holmes's famous methods of observation and inference in action: his use of tape measure and magnifying lens, his identification of tobacco ashes, his interpretation of wheel tracks, hoof marks and footprints, and the

The first meeting of Sherlock Holmes and Dr Watson in the chemical laboratory of St Bartholomew's Hospital, London, as depicted by George Hutchinson in an early edition of *A Study in Scarlet*. The foppish figure in topper and spats is Watson!

characteristically downright, positive yet at the same time faultlessly grammatical language in which he conveys his decisions and his conclusions — language indeed, whose accuracy is itself a tribute to Conan Doyle's schooling at Stoneyhurst, which reads so well on the page but which is nevertheless extraordinarily difficult to bring off convincingly in actual speech, and which almost always defeats the efforts of pastiche writers to create a credible imitation of it:

"The murderer was a man. He was more than six feet high, was in the prime of life, had small feet for his height, wore coarse, square-toed boots and smoked a Trichinopoly cigar. He came here with his victim in a four-wheeled cab, which was drawn by a horse with three old shoes and one new one on his off fore-leg. In all probability the murderer had a florid face, and the finger-nails of his right hand were remarkably long. These are only a few indications, but they may assist you".

As to Holmes's appearance, we are given Watson's description of him:

"In height he was rather over six feet, and so excessively lean that he seemed to be considerably taller. His eyes were sharp and piercing, save during those intervals of torpor to which I have alluded; and his thin, hawk-like nose gave his whole expression an air of alertness and decision"

— but no firm pictorial representation of the great detective emerges from this first account of his adventures. The action takes place in London. At home in Baker Street he likes to be comfortable in his dressing gown, but out of doors he would wear morning dress or a less formal suit, with topper or Homburg as the case may be. He certainly does not career about the streets of the metropolis in a caped coat and deerstalker. Several other of his well known eccentricities, such as the odd stowage for his tobacco and cigars, do not appear in this tale. He does not yet inject himself with cocaine. He does not say "Elementary, my dear Watson".

Dr Doyle was pleased with his detective story, and well he might have been. "I knew that the book was as good as I could make it," he wrote, "and I had high hopes". Alas, the fate of *A Study In Scarlet* is only too well known. After several rejections it was finally accepted in October that year by Messrs Ward Lock & Company who offered £25 for the copyright outright (less even, than he had got for *Habakuk Jephson*), with the proviso that they could not publish it for another year or so, when they might find a place for it in one of their Annuals. Fed up, the author agreed; "I never made another penny from it".

With the book completed and sent off, he characteristically turned his restless mind to other matters. Portsmouth that summer was in the grip of election fever, and although he was never a party politician by nature, Dr Doyle was one of those people who could never resist entering an argument, or taking up a cause, and once he had done so, playing it for all he was worth. Since one of the main issues of the election was Ireland, he had found it impossible to stay out. The two main parties were the Conservatives of Lord Salisbury and the Liberals led by Mr Gladstone. The Conservatives were the party of the aristocracy, the landed proprietors, country gentlemen, entrepreneurs, businessmen and shopkeepers — the Empire builders. Hampshire was a highly Conservative county. The member for South Hampshire was General Sir Frederick Fitz-Wygram, Bart; a cavalry officer, former Colonel in the 3rd Hussars — he couldn't be anything but a Conservative. The Liberals comprised most of the rest of the voters — there was no Labour party to speak of. Portsmouth was something of a Liberal stronghold, with a very active Liberal Association under the Chairmanship of Mr John Pares JP. Mr Gladstone's party, however, had an offshoot. One of the main items in his policy was Home Rule for Ireland; that is, he advocated a separate Parliament for Ireland (the whole of which at that time was part of the United Kingdom) as the only practical means of ending "the troubles". A good many Liberals, however, did not subscribe to this view, but felt instead, with the Conservatives, that Ireland should remain in the same status as

The "received" British image of Sherlock Holmes drawn by the artist Sidney Paget, showing the detective in his country travelling outfit of long caped coat and deerstalker hat.

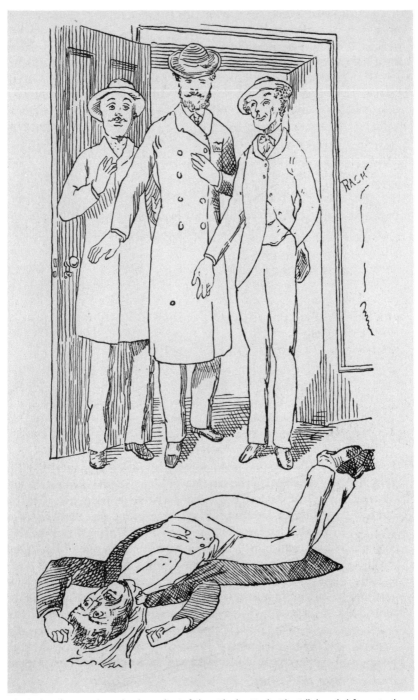

Sherlock Holmes as drawn by the author's father, Charles Doyle. The tall, bearded figure in the centre is much more akin to Charles Doyle himself than to his son's description of Holmes.

Scotland and Wales, in union with the mother country. They called themselves Liberal-Unionists, therefore.

Conan Doyle, notwithstanding his Irish antecedents, was as we have seen a great Empire man, and saw himself firmly on the side of the Liberal-Unionists. He soon found himself elected a Vice-Chairman of the local branch, and he set out his views with typical clarity in a letter to the *Evening News* on 6 July:

"Sir, As a man holding liberal opinions upon many of the leading questions of the day, I should like to explain why I and many more are about to vote for the Unionist candidate. The whole controversy may, it appears to me, be summed up in the following six propositions, which I have never heard controverted:

1. That since the year 1881 the agitation in Ireland has been characterised by a long succession of crimes against life and property.

2. That these murders and maimings have never been heartily denounced by any member of the Irish parliamentary party.

3. That politicians who could allow such deeds to be done without raising their voices against them cannot be men of high political morality — and are, therefore, however talented, unfit to be trusted with the destinies of a country.

4. That Michael Davitt, whose influence in Ireland is hardly second to that of Parnell, has publicly stated that this shall *not* be a final settlement.

5. That Ireland ought to have in justice the same privileges as England, Scotland or Wales, but that there is no reason why she should have more than these three law-abiding countries.

6. That a grand scheme of Imperial Federation is nearly ripe, by which every country should manage its own local affairs, leaving Imperial matters to a central Parliament, in which every division of the Empire should be represented. That any exceptional Irish legislation of the nature proposed would hamper this just and symmetrical design, which we owe largely to the genius of that eniment Radical, the late Mr W.E. Forster.

I trust that by publishing this short statement you may give another proof of that good feeling which has characterised this political campaign. If we differ from men whose opinions we share on many other subjects, it is not from any narrow class or party feeling, but from an honest conviction that an Irish Parliament would not conduce to the strength and prosperity of that Empire which all parties are anxious to uphold.

I remain, Sir, sincerely yours,
A. Conan Doyle".

This clean-cut image of Holmes with pipe and dressing-gown is by his most famous American delineator, Frederick Dorr Steele.

In *Memories And Adventures* he relates how, at one of the pre-election meetings, the candidate was delayed so he himself was pushed on to the platform to address an audience of three thousand:

"It was one of the tight corners of my life. I hardly knew myself what I said, but the Irish part of me came to my aid and supplied me with a torrent of more or less incoherent words and similes which roused the audience greatly, though it read to me afterwards more like a comic stump speech than a serious effort".

Somehow I think Conan Doyle is being a little overmodest here. He was a good talker, never one to hold back his own views, with a strong sense of mission fuelling any public activity he undertook. Besides, it can be far easier to whip up enthusiasm among a large crowd with a few boldy expressed half-truths repeated ad nauseam, as many a political and trade union leader has found out, than to convince a much smaller but more critical body. The following anecdote, taken from the same source, seems to me to display his character more directly:

"I was acting Secretary when Mr Balfour came down to address a great meeting and, as such, when the Hall was full, I waited on the curb outside to receive him. Presently his carriage drove up and out he stepped, tall, thin and aristocratic. There were two notorious partisans of the other side waiting for him and I warned them not to make trouble. However, the moment Balfour appeared one of them opened a huge mouth with the intention of emitting a howl of execration. But it never got out, for I clapped my hand pretty forcibly over the orifice while I held him by the neck with the other hand. His companion hit me on the head with a stick, and was promptly knocked down by one of my companions. Meanwhile Balfour got safely in, and we two secretaries followed, rather dishevelled after our adventure. I met Lord Balfour several times in after life but I never told him how I once had my hat smashed in his defence".

So much for "that good feeling which has characterised this campaign"! Would that some of our popular and too noisy demos today could be controlled so effectively.

The *Evening News* itself was straight Liberal. In the same issue the editorial stated:

"Those who are capable of putting personal considerations altogether on one side, and taking a broad view of the present struggle, will feel in no humour to play the game of the so-called Unionists... We trust that our local Liberals will do their duty".

(They might have said, in Nelson's home port, "The News expects. . . ")

"We hope to have the gratification of announcing tomorrow another great Liberal victory in the good old town".

In the event, nevertheless, the other side carried the day, and at the count the two sitting members, General Sir William Crossman (Liberal-Unionist) and Sir Samuel Wilson (Conservative) were returned. One of the losing Liberal candidates was Alderman John Baker, founder of the tailoring business J. Baker & Company, familiar to several generations of Navy men. Nationally the Conservatives got in, and Lord Salisbury became Prime Minister, disappointingly for Conan Doyle's plain man-in-the-street politics, so tidily and hopefully expressed. The Empire has been and gone and Ireland has got her Parliament, but the "crimes against life and property" seem to go on just the same.

There was cricket as usual that summer. The Australians — in those days known as the Colonists — were touring England, but the *Portsmouth Times* still found space to report the results of local matches. Dr Doyle played regularly from mid-May onwards, scoring quite consistently too; he made 22, 41,42 and 25 in successive games. Then playing away against Fareham on 23 June he got nought in both innings — the dreaded pair of spectacles, clean bowled both times. Hayter and Welsh both got among the runs as well, and Hemingsley was the most effective bowler, but poor Dr Weston, one of the founder members, seems unfortunately to have been squeezed out of the first team by this time. Norman Pares, playing for the Grammar School masters against the Royal Naval College (which was then in the Dockyard) made no less than 127.

The other main civic event of the year was probably the laying of the foundation stone of the new Town Hall on Thursday 14 October by the Mayor, Alderman A.S. Blake. The Town Council, looking ahead with commendable enterprise to the need to replace the old Hall in the High Street, had bought the site near the Town station from the War Department, owners of so much desirable land in Portsmouth, as far back as 1883. The imposing design with its great pillared and porticoed front bore a stiking resemblance to that of Leeds Town Hall in Yorkshire, which is perhaps not so surprising since the architect was a Leeds man, William Hill. The estimate for the construction, also by a Leeds firm, was £98,245.

In September the distinguished American preacher and anti-slavery campaigner, the Reverend Henry Ward Beecher, paid a visit to Portsmouth (He was a brother of Harriet Beecher Stowe, the author of *Uncle Tom's Cabin*). He was to give a lecture on "The Wastes and Burdens of Society" at the King Street Chapel, Portsea, and a large audience was expected. In the event however his reception was disappointing. As the *Evening News* reported on 25 September:

> "There was but a small attendance, a result stated to be due to the action of some of the ministers of religion of the borough, who advised their congregations to stay away, and indeed to 'Boycott' the lecture".

One seems to feel the hand of the fiery Reverend Lindsay Young behind this anti-Beecher movement; no doubt he would be out of sympathy with the visitor's Congregational attachment.

The Mayor presided at the meeting but we do not know whether Dr Doyle was present. Sherlockians, though, will remember that H.W. Beecher was one of Dr Watson's heroes; he kept an unframed portrait of the preacher above his desk at 221B.

On 25 October the citizens of Southsea were treated to a recital by the Russian pianist Vladimir de Pachmann, an artist famous for his interpretations of Chopin and notorious for his habit of carrying on little conversations with himself during his performances. Some of his old records can still be found. The concert was:

> "thoroughly enjoyed by the audience, and evidently, if appearances are not misleading, by the eminent pianist himself"

reported the *Evening News*; perhaps the great man indulged himself in one of his little chats on this occasion too. Did the gentle Louise persuade her husband to take her along? Perhaps not. "Sorry, my dear. Evening surgery, you know". A few rousing choruses in the Bush or the Blue Anchor would be more in the doctor's line. Still, she could always go with her mother.

The concert was held in the Portland Hall, which stood at the end of Kent Road, just past the Portland Hotel. It was arranged, as these musical events usually were, by Mr C.E. Godfrey, who had a piano and music business in the town. It would be interesting to know if he was related to Sir Dan Godfrey, the well known music director and conductor of the Bournemouth Municipal Orchestra.

September brought the first practice games of football, and by mid-October the season was in full swing. A new competition had been instituted for a Portsmouth and District Challenge Cup, which had been provided largely as a result of the money-raising efforts of Robert Hemingsley. Ten teams entered for the first round: Portsmouth, Woolston (the strong side from the Southampton boat-building works), Hilsea Ramblers (a Royal Artillery team), Portsmouth Grammar School, Hayling Island, Petersfield, Cowes, Horndean, the Sunflowers, and Freemantle (a Gosport side). The first four all won easily, Portsmouth beating Petersfield 6-1, but Sunflowers unfortunately had to scratch at the last minute. The inclusion of the Grammar School looks surprising, since the school game had formerly been rugger; no doubt the influence of Norman Pares, who as we have already seen had played at back once or twice with the Portsmouth side, had much to do with the decision to change over to soccer, and the Grammar has been a soccer school ever since.

Dr Doyle got a brief notice once in his professional capacity, with this note in the *Evening News* of 26 November:

> "Sudden death. Yesterday Dr Conan Doyle was called to Lizzie Kate Slatterie, 5, at 31 Green Road, Southsea, but death had taken place before his arrival. The Coroner has decided not to hold an inquest".

Just another child death, one feels, only too common in those times; croup, whooping cough, measles, or one of the fevers.

The following week there was an accident which he missed:

> "Alfred Gray, 9 years of age, of 9 Boulton Road, Southsea, accidentally slipped while carrying a child in Elm Grove, and having his thigh fractured, he was conveyed to the hospital and detained for treatment".

No doubt he would have been ready enough to see to the little boy had his attention been drawn to the incident, but the days of sitting at his window hoping for just an eventuality were well behind him now.

Dr Weston featured in an inquest at about this time. Thomas Johns, aged 41, a naval pensioner and dockyard labourer of Hertford Street, Landport, had been found dead in the street while on his way to work at 5.15 one morning. About two years previously he had had an attack of pleurisy, since when he had been attended by Dr Weston who, according to the report, "told deceased that he was dying fast, and could not live long". Dr Weston may have given this bedside advice in his usual cheery manner, but it can hardly have had the same effect on his patient!

The Literary Society opened its new season on 9 November under the Presidency of General Cox, with Dr Doyle now acting as joint Secretary with Dr Cousins. Among the new members was Mr W.H. Handley, proprietor of the famous drapery store at the corner of Palmerston Road and Osborne Road. The shop was destroyed by bombs and rebuilt in the 1950s, and though it has now been taken over by a big multiple the site is still known to shoppers and bus drivers as Handley's corner. Another famous name to join was Mr John Brickwood, who was then living at 13 Clarendon Road. Later, as his business empire expanded and he became Sir John, he moved to "Byculla", an enormous mock-Tudor extravaganza on the north side of Kent Road standing in a huge garden complete with an ornamental lake. This house later became a girl's private school, then a Police headquarters, and later still, with its beautiful grounds to waste, a set of Social Security offices. The name of Brickwood is famous to many generations of Pompey naval men. He was the manufacturer of Brickwood's Brilliant Ales, a firm which, rather like the Pinks' grocery empire, steadily expanded to absorb most of its rivals in the town, only to be taken over in its turn by an even bigger national conglomerate in the 1970s. The name is still there, in its elaborate curly lettering, on many of Pompey's tiled pub fronts.

One other new member whom I cannot resist mentioning was the splendidly named Le Vicomte B. de Pobong-Dmochovski, of Avoca Lodge, Freestone Road, Southsea. I hope he told the Secretaries how to pronounce it before they introduced him.

General Cox opened the proceedings with his Presidential address on "Recent Progress in Some Branches of Science", in which, understandably enough, he managed to bring his talk round to the subject of military weaponry:

> "The country would insist that our small army, relatively, should be possessed of the best possible weapons to enable it when called upon — and the time might not be far distant — to defend the safety, honour, and integrity of the British Empire."

(Loud applause from all two hundred present).

General Drayson featured no less than twice, even before Christmas, with more about the Ecliptic and his pet theory of the Second Rotation of the Earth. Neither of his pieces generated any serious discussion from his audience, who must have been thoroughly blinded with science by now. The other speaker was Percy Boulnois, the Borough Engineer, on "A Few Facts about Money", a talk which led him on to the subject of the Bimetallic Question, a somewhat theoretical problem relating to the use of both gold and silver as dual standards of currency. In the discussion Dr James Watson was moved to remark feelingly how the depreciation in the value of silver was the means of causing considerable loss to those who received their pensions in India (and China too, no doubt).

Dr Doyle, as a conscientious secretary, attended every meeting; and it may be no coincidence that one of the topics on which Mycroft Holmes, Sherlock's civil servant brother, is found to be an expert, is the Bimetallic Question.

CHAPTER **VI**

1887 - Oculism and Occultism

WE ARE NOW roughly half way through Dr Doyle's term as a resident of Southsea. Gone are the days — they did not last all that long — of cooking saveloys over a gas jet in his back kitchen, sneaking out at night to polish his brass plate, keeping the precious pounds for his rent locked away in his desk drawer; long gone, but not of course forgotten, any more than any of us ever forgets his early struggles. In the short space of four years he had come a long way. He had built himself up a nice little business from nothing, enough now to give him a moderately comfortable living, at least free from serious financial worries and yet with enough spare time in which to pursue his other interests. He had got a nice little house, now decently furnished, and a nice little wife to share it with him and provide the basis of a stable domestic routine, so invaluable both to his professional position and to his own energetic temperament. He had got his name into the paper, any number of times. He had had a book accepted; not yet published, it is true, and for a derisory payment, but accepted it was, and therefore off his mind, even if *The Firm Of Girdlestone & Co* was still drawing blank on its rounds. He had his new degree, and was now properly entitled to the designation "Doctor", which previously, though commonly used, was strictly only a courtesy title for those who did not have an MD. The Army List of the period, for example, was quite punctilious in this. Surgeon officers with only the basic degree of MB were referred to as "Mr". Only those, like Surgeon Major Evatt, with an MD to their name were listed as "Dr". And, he was known. People recognised him as they passed him in the street. He had made friends among all classes of Portsmouth society through his activities in sport, literature and politics as well as his profession — as much for his personal qualities as for any of his undoubted abilities, as the Vice-President of the Bowling Club had said at his presentation party. The fact was, people liked him; a big man, big in heart as well as physique, a great talker, equally happy in pub, domestic circle, lecture hall or committee room, fond of a story (and more so if he was able to cap it himself) — he could feel assured of a welcome in any company.

Of course, he still took his profession very seriously. One illustration of his case work at this time is given by an item held in St Mary's

Hospital Postgraduate Centre. It is his bill for attendance on the sick wife of a Mr W. Chapman, of 91 Cottage Grove, a street of mixed class to the north of Elm Grove, only a few minutes' walk from Bush Villa. Between 3 February and 7 April he visited Mrs Chapman no fewer than 38 times, often calling on four or five days in succession. His bill came to £7-11s-6d (£7.58p). Allowing for 16 bottles of medicine (unfortunately not effective; the poor patient died, but perhaps they helped to ease her sufferings), this works out at approximately 3/6d (17½ p) per visit.

Mrs Chapman's husband may have been partly consoled in the thought that he had at least been able to afford his doctor's bill — modest as it may seem to us today — for such constant attendance on his wife during her last illness. There were a great many people in the town who could not. Two years previously a group of citizens led by Admiral Sir G. Phipps Hornby had succeeded in raising enough money from donations and subscriptions to found the beginnings of a District Nursing organisation in Portsmouth. By February 1885 they had enough to rent No 8 Gloucester Terrace (a little street running into Elm Grove near Green Road) at £38 a year and to employ two full-time nurses and a lady superintendent whose combined salaries came to £90-16s-8d. This was the Borough of Portsmouth Association for Nursing the Sick Poor. Dr Claremont was one of the Honorary

No 91, Cottage Grove, Southsea, shown with alterations in progress in 1985. Mrs Chapman, a patient of Dr Doyle, lived here in 1887.   (Photo: R.F. Reynolds, Cosham).

Secretaries, and there was also a Naval Surgeon, Dr E.S. Woods, on the committee. Dr Watson became a subscriber (5 shillings a year), as did many others, but the real heroines of the Association must have been the two working nurses, Miss Lander and Miss Mitchel. They were provided with their keep at Gloucester Terrace, but must have received less than £1 a week each in wages. Here are two typically desperate examples from their case notes:

"Mrs B. . ., aged 26, (suffering in consequence of the ignorant treatment of an unqualified midwife) the wife of a soldier, having three very young children and no relative or neighbour to help her. When we first opened the door of the room (sic) she lodged in, and not knowing what the case was, we thought the patient must be mad, as the room was littered with straw, coal, firewood, ashes and broken crockery. The woman was standing in her night gown with an old shawl round her head, another on her shoulders, mittens on her hands and an Army blanket half on her and half trailing on the ground. When we asked her why she was out of bed she said there was nobody to keep the children from doing mischief and that she had been nearly out of her mind with their noise and the baby crying so because there had been no one to wash or dress him for days, but that getting out of bed made her have the 'cold shivers' so badly. We found fresh straw had been put in the bed ticking but the end had not been sewn up; so, when we had done that we swept the room, took away a quantity of ashes from the grate, collected out of cupboards and corners all the soiled linen and clothes we could find and made arrangements to have them washed. Washed and dressed 2 children, aged 3 and 18 months, washed and dressed baby, got all shawls off patient, sponged her, cleared up all crocks etc off table and left. In the evening the husband was home, expressed much gratitude and promised to wash floor that night. Next day was Christmas but he had leave the following day, would then scrub it. Found a kind woman to look after 2 youngsters for the day". (Later report: convalescing).

Miss. . . . When we first visited this patient we found her suffering from Cancer of breast, shoulder and arm, also Jaundice. Patient told us she had been ill for more than three years, and had been under two operations. Her friends who were very good and kind had been able to attend to her, but now she had become so bad they could neither change the sheets nor properly bathe the wounds, and she would feel most thankful if we would come and do it for her. We found the Cancer had spread from the breast under the arm to back and shoulder, the right arm which was resting upon a pillow looked about three times its natural size, and was fractured above the elbow. After washing her we cleaned and dressed wounds as ordered, changed the sheets, arranged hair, took precautions against bedsores, and left her as she said was feeling quite comfortable. A few days after this she had the misfortune to fracture her thigh, which was much diseased. For nearly a fortnight afterwards she was in such great pain she would not have the sheets changed without the doctor first administrating ether, but as this made her very ill all the next day and prevented her taking her nourishment, we at last persuaded her to let us try and change them without ether, this we succeeded in doing without causing her any additional pain".

(Later report: Death).

Any other man in Dr Doyle's place might well have considered he had made satisfactory progress to date, but not he. Somehow, his restless energy and enquiring mind drove him to seek further outlets, to make wider contacts. Besides, although his practice was by now steady enough it was not really getting any bigger. The MD didn't seem to have made all that difference — certainly not to the majority of his patients, who still came from the poorer parts of Southsea. He could still compare himself unfavourably with Dr James Watson, for example. For, the Reverend Tompkins having been promoted to be Vicar of St Peter's in Somers Road and in consequence moved his family into his new vicarage, Dr Watson had seized his chance and moved up into Elmwood, that nice Owen house just off Elm Grove which had so conveniently been vacated; a property which approximated far more nearly to the fictitious Mrs Esdaile's "pretty house and charming grounds" than ever Bush Villa could. Moreover, Dr James had got himself on to the Committee of the Ladies Nursing Home in Granada Road, thereby adding a useful hundred or two to his practice income. It was not that Dr Doyle was discontented — I would not suggest that. But I'm sure that he felt he could still do better.

So, to use a contemporary expression, he diversified. His first new venture this year was to become a Freemason. On 26 January he was initiated into Phoenix Lodge, No 257 at 110 High Street (there were sixteen Masonic Lodges in Portsmouth, as well as various branches of the Buffaloes, the Oddfellows, Royal Arch Chapters, and similar organisations). His sponsors were Mr W.D. King, a former Mayor (later Sir William David King, Deputy Lieutenant of Hampshire), and John Brickwood. Whether he first evinced an interest in Freemasonry because of its charitable activities, or because he felt it might help to fill the gap in the religious side of his life, or because it achieved a further widening of his social circle, a chance to meet some more of the town's big men, it is impossible to tell. Possibly all three. Obviously such a well known local sportsman and professional man would have been greeted as a welcome addition to any Lodge, but on the whole

Elm Grove in Conan Doyle's time. A view taken looking west from the junction with Grove Road (where the traffic lights are now). Dr Watson's house "Elmwood" is hidden behind the trees in the left foreground (now the site of Telephone House).

Freemasonry seems to have been something of a disappointment to him. He resigned from the Lodge two years later, while still a resident of Southsea. He did rejoin some fifteen years afterwards when he was living at Hindhead, and in 1901 accepted honorary membership of St Mary's Chapel No 1, Edinburgh, but he resigned again from the Southsea Lodge without taking any of the higher degrees in the Craft.

Conan Doyle never wrote seriously about Freemasonry in any of his works, and did not mention it at all in his autobiography. There are occasional references to Freemasons in the Holmes canon, but only in brief general terms or as a means of identifying an individual. Thus Enoch J. Drebber, the murder victim in *A Study In Scarlet*, is found to have "a gold ring with Masonic device" among all his possessions. "There is a wonderful sympathy and freemasonry among horsey men", remarks Holmes in *A Scandal in Bohemia*, the first of the *Strand* short stories. In a much later adventure, *The Norwood Builder*, we have the following typical sally from Holmes on meeting his new client John Hector McFarlane for the first time:

"You mentioned your name as if I should recognise it, but I assure you that, beyond obvious facts that you are a bachelor, a solicitor, a Freemason, and an asthmatic, I know nothing whatever about you".

Watson, by then fairly well up in Holmes's methods, had already noticed the visitor's Masonic watch-chain himself.

By 1887 Dr Doyle was also making serious forays into the mysteries of Spiritualism. The problem which nagged him — and many other Victorian men, of greater scientific achievement than himself — and which formed the basis of some of his religious doubts, was whether it might be possible to obtain tangible evidence, in the shape of some physical manifestation or otherwise, that a man's mind (or spirit, or soul) could be shown to exist independently of his body. His medical instructors had assured him that this was impossible, and he had accepted this:

> "I had at that time the usual contempt which the young educated man feels towards the whole subject which has been covered by the clumsy name of Spiritualism".

Nevertheless the doubt was still there at the back of his mind. He had already taken part in some crude experiments in telepathy with Henry Ball, a fellow-member of the Literary Society who was in private practice as an architect at 2 Portland Place (another long-vanished house on Kent Road, near St Jude's Church). The two men sat in chairs one behind the other. One would draw a simple diagram, and attempt "mentally" to describe it to the other who would then draw in his turn. "Again and again, " Dr Doyle wrote, ". . .he in turn has made approximately the same figure".

There is some doubt about the actual date of his first psychic experiments. John Dickson Carr, who had access to all Conan Doyle's private papers before they became locked up in litigation, gives an exact date: "The sittings began on 24 January 1887, and went on at intervals until the beginning of July" — but this refers to some sittings with Henry Ball, at which occasionally an experienced medium named Horstead was present. Conan Doyle himself (who, like Holmes's Watson, was not always absolutely accurate about dates) twice quotes the year 1886: in his book *The New Revelation*, published in 1918:

> "I met some friends, however, who are interested in the matter, and I sat with them at some table-moving seances. . .About this time — it would be in 1886. . ."

and, six years later, in *Memories and Adventures*:

> "About this time (1886) the family of a General whom I attended professionally became interested in table turning and asked me to come and check their results".

Nor can we be sure that these two items refer to the same set of sittings. The latter must refer to General Drayson, but who are the "some friends" in the former — Drayson, Ball, or somebody else? None of Conan Doyle's biographies has noticed that he also took part in experimental seances with some members of the Ford family. Douglas Morey Ford, a solicitor, was an elder brother of Arthur Vernon Ford, the ophthalmic surgeon. Like Dr Doyle he had literary ambitions, and had indeed published two early novels, and it may be through this connection that Doyle met the brother Vernon. Or it may have been the other way round (neither Douglas nor Vernon Ford was a member of the Literary Society, though another brother, Archibald was). It was Douglas's wife Honor, however, who held the table turning sessions in their home at No 1 Grand Parade. A history of the Ford family compiled by a descendant R.A. Parker gives a brief account of one of these which is not without its comic side:

> "It would have been about 1885 that D (i.e. Douglas) and his family made the acquaintance of Arthur Conan Doyle. It is well known that Conan Doyle was extremely interested in psychic phenomena and a number of sessions of 'table turning' took place at D's house, when his wife Honor and her family and friends participated with Doyle and his circle. D did not believe in spiritualism and indeed frowned on the practice. There is a family story that on one occasion when a session of 'table turning' was in progress, and the table was apparently of its own volition heading out of the door, D arrived home and was incensed to find what was going on, and did not mince his words. Presumably any interruption of the friendship between the two families was only short-lived, as the family still maintained contacts many years later. . ."

Quite possibly the early date given, 1885, is also inexact. All three references tend to confirm, however, that Dr Doyle did not take part actively in spiritualist experiments until after he was married, and consequently raises the interesting question, was Louise herself a member of "Doyle and his circle"? There seems no reason to suppose that she was not. Young Victorian ladies, after all, were no less curious about their futures — before or after death — than their successors are today. More seriously, both Louise and her mother had suffered a double bereavement in recent times, with the loss of father and brother, husband and son, within six months of one another. Hopes of a "communication" from "the other side" may not have been far from the thoughts of either of them. Besides, there seems to have been a pleasant air of domesticity about Mrs Ford's afternoon sessions, with tea and cakes well in evidence, surely. Louise certainly remained a friend of the family, and was godmother to the Ford's younger daughter, Delia.

Dr Doyle himself, however, would soon tire of these teacup-reading sessions with their leavening of romantic overtones and gossip. Spirit communication was a serious subject and should be taken seriously in

Grand Parade, Old Portsmouth. Conan Doyle attended some early spiritualist sessions at No 1, Grand Parade, the home of the solicitor Douglas Morey Ford and his wife Honor. No 1 is the third from the left, now restored with balconies added.

a man's world. It is no wonder that he readily accepted an invitation to take part in a series of seances at 20 Ashburton road, General Drayson's home. He had, indeed, a lot of time for the General. Quite apart from the natural respect he no doubt felt towards a man much older than himself with a distinguished Army career behind him, he had obviously seen a lot of him at the Literary Society. Drayson was an intellectual, an astronomer and a scientist, who knew about things like the binomial theorem and the obliquity of the ecliptic. You had to respect the views of a man like that. He had made conscientious efforts to follow the General's own patent theory of the Second Rotation of the Earth — though we may take leave to doubt whether he did understand it fully. (A good many others did not; all through January and February the correspondence columns of the *Portsmouth Times* were filled with critical letters from others of his listeners, and lengthy replies from Drayson defending himself. One gentleman, a Mr John Hampden of Bosham, who seems to have been a member of the Flat Earth Society, wrote, "Never mind the second one. Has he any proof of the earth's first rotation?"). Besides, both men were keen billiard players, and may well have had the odd hundred up together on one of Mr Hill's excellent tables at the Bush (Holmes's Watson was fond of a game, too). So Doctor Doyle must have felt quite flattered when, at some time in the previous year, Drayson had asked him in for a professional consultation; senior Army officers did not feature largely in the sick parade at Bush Villa.

General Drayson's psychic sessions seem, at this stage at least, to have been of a no more elaborate nature than those at Grand Parade (though possibly the company was a bit too senior for Louise this time):

> "They sat round a dining-room table which after a time, their hands being upon it, began to sway and finally got sufficient motion to tap with one leg. They then asked questions and received answers, more or less wise and more or less to the point. They were got by the tedious process of reciting the alphabet and writing down the letter which the tap indicated. It seemed to me that we were collectively pushing the table, and that our own wills were concerned in bringing down the leg at the right moment. I was interested but very sceptical"
>
> *(Memories and Adventures).*

Conan Doyle referred to these early sittings again in *The New Revelation*; but it is hard not to feel that even then, for all the supposed spiritual origin of the messages, his own reactions remained remarkably earthbound:

> "Messages. . . were not always absolutely stupid. For example, I find that on one occasion, on my asking some test question, such as how many coins I had in my pocket, the table spelt out, "We are here to educate and to elevate, not to guess riddles".

Or again:

> "We had very good conditions" — (what were they?) — "one evening, and an amount of movement which seemed quite independent of our pressure. Long and detailed messages came through, which purported to be from a spirit who gave his name, and said he was a commercial traveller who had lost his life in a recent fire at a theatre in Exeter. All the details were exact, and he implored us to write to his family who lived, he said, at a place called Slattenmere, in Cumberland. I did so, but my letter came back, appropriately enough, through the dead letter office (!). . . If there is such a place as Slattenmere in the world I should even now be glad to know it".

There is the village of Satterthwaite, near Hawkeshead, but no Slattenmere.

It is difficult, writing in 1985, not to feel superior, let alone cynical, about some of the detail in the following report, also from *The New Revelation:*

"Two communicators sent messages, the first of whom spelt out as a name 'Dorothy Postlethwaite', a name unknown to any of us. She said she died at Melbourne, five years before, at the age of sixteen, that she was now happy... that the sphere she inhabited was all round the earth; that she knew about the planets; that Mars was inhabited by a race more advanced than us, and that the canals were artificial... she was still a Catholic, but had not fared better than the Protestants; there were Buddhists and Mohammedans in her sphere, but all fared alike; she had never seen Christ and knew no more about Him than on earth, but believed in His influence; spirits prayed and they died in their new sphere before entering another..." etc.

Conan Doyle kept a record in a notebook of his Southsea sittings, but at that time at least, and notwithstanding General Drayson's persuasiveness, he says he remained firmly sceptical:

"I never received anything evidential to my own address, and I was very critical as to the whole proceedings."

Privately he felt that all the so-called spirit messages could be explained as the effects of telepathy. He did not carry out any seances himself ("I was too poor to employ professional mediums"), and in any case has left it on record that his conversion did not take place until as late as 1916. It was the enormous casualty lists of the War, in which he himself lost his brother Innes — the cheery companion of his first years in Southsea — and his eldest son Kingsley, which finally convinced him of the call to carry out his great message of consolation to all the world's bereaved; or so we are led to suppose.

Nevertheless, at the conclusion of his 1887 experiments he wrote a letter to the weekly periodical *Light* ("A Journal of Psychical, Occult and Mystical Research, edited by 'M.A.(Oxon)' and E. Dawson Rogers") which suggests that he was by no means as sceptical as his other writings might indicate. Published in the issue dated 2 July under the title "A Test Message", it begins:

"Sir, I believe that it has been found a useful practice among revivalists and other excitable religionists of all types, for each member to give the assembled congregation a description of the manner in which they attained the somewhat vague result known as 'finding salvation'... This must be my apology, therefore, for dwelling upon the incident which, after many months of inquiry, showed me at last that it was absolutely certain that intelligence could exist apart from the body".

After describing his dissatisfaction with table-turning, including sessions with a circle of six which met nine or ten times at his own house, he goes on to relate the details of one of his sittings with the medium Horstead. Prior to this he had been debating with himself whether or not he should read a particular book, *Comic Dramatists of the Restoration*, by Leigh Hunt — something which no one else could possibly have known. The letter continues:

"Last week I was invited by two friends to join them in a sitting with an old gentleman who was reputed to have considerable mediumistic power. It was the first time I had ever had the opportunity of sitting with anyone who was not a novice and inquirer like myself. . . On sitting, our medium came quickly under control, and delivered a trance address, containing much interesting and elevating material. He then became clairvoyant, describing one or two scenes which we had no opportunity of testing. . . We then proposed writing. The medium took up a pencil, and after a few convulsive movements, he wrote a message to each of us. Mine ran: 'This gentleman is a healer. Tell him from me not to read Leigh Hunt's book'. . . I can only say that if I had had to devise a test message I could not have hit upon one which was so absolutely inexplicable on any hypothesis except that held by Spiritualists. . . "

To my mind, however, the letter is more remarkable for its concluding paragraph, in which the writer sets out a powerful statement of his own personal philosophy:

"Above all, let any inquirer bear in mind that phenomena are only a means to an end, of no value at all of themselves, and simply useful as giving us assurance of an after existence for which we are to prepare by refining away our grosser animal feelings and cultivating our higher, nobler impulses. . . Let a man realise that the human soul, as it emerges from its bodily cocoon, shapes its destiny in exact accordance with its condition; that that condition depends upon the sum result of his actions and thoughts in this life; that every evil deed stamps itself upon the spirit and entails its own punishment with the same certainty that a man stepping out of a second floor window falls to the ground; that there is no room for deathbed repentances or other nebulous conditions which might screen the evil doer from the consequences of his own deeds, but that the law is self-acting and inexorable. . . This, I take it, is the lesson which Spritualism enforces".

Neither *Light* nor any of its correspondents offered any comment on this outspoken letter. The following month Conan Doyle wrote to *Light* again. On 13 August the paper ran a paragraph warning spiritualists against the activities of an investigator called Richard Hodgson, who was said to be touring Europe and America with the express intention of exposing all mediums as fraudulent, the genuine as well as the fake ones. On 20 August it published a letter from a correspondent signing himself "A Student" opposing such warnings; if a medium was genuine, what had he to fear from any investigation? Conan Doyle immediately wrote in support:

> "As a Spiritualist, I for one should like to see every possible facility given to Mr Hodgson in his investigations. If Spiritualism be true and the phenomena genuine, why should the mediums be warned against Mr Hodgson or any other inquirer? Far from throwing difficulties in Mr Hodgson's way, a fund might well be set on foot by Spiritualists to assist him in cleaning out the Augean stables of professional mediumship".

In *Memories and Adventures* Conan Doyle is mildly sceptical about the Horstead sitting:

> "This then was a very final and excellent test so far as telepathy went, but I would not fully grant that it was more".

The intriguing question as to who might have been the originator of the message ("Tell him from *me*. . .") is left unanswered. However, the expression "As a Spiritualist" at the beginning of his letter of 20 August would seem to show that already at Southsea he was much farther along the road to spiritualism than he would have us believe.

Back to the open air. It was another hard winter, with snow and severe storms in the first week of January, and more of the same as late as the middle of March. In fact the eighties and nineties generally were a time of harsh winters in Britain, that of 1895 being the worst of the century. Nevertheless the Portsmouth Football Club achieved another successful tally of 25 matches won out of 33 played, and 87 to 30 in goals. Lancelot Pares, playing at centre forward or inside left, got no fewer than 34 of these:

> "his dash, dribbling and shooting being quite a treat. Indeed his performances this season fairly entitle him to be regarded as the best forward player in the district"

wrote the *Evening News*. In one match against a team from HMS Marlborough three of the Pares brothers were in the Portsmouth side. "A.C. Smith" again exploited his heavy punting as goalkeeper or at right back, but he did miss one or two games in January and February. He was not playing when the club lost 1-3 away to Wimborne in the semi-final of the Hants and Dorset cup; an important match, and a hard decision to make, but he was attending Mrs Chapman at this time and obviously could not spare the whole day away from the practice (unlike Dr Watson in London, who was always happy to leave his patients in the care of his neighbours Jackson or Anstruther whenever Holmes had an interesting case on).

The highlight of the season was undoubtedly the final of the new Portsmouth and District Challenge Cup on 26 March, between Portsmouth and their old rivals Woolston Works (who had already won the Hants and Dorset Cup, and defeated Hilsea Ramblers 8-0 in the second round). Portsmouth had got there by beating the Grammar School 3-0 in the second round and Freemantle 2-0 in the semi-final. The match was played in front of a large and excited crowd on the United Services Recreation Ground. Portsmouth put out a full team with "Smith" in goal, Peters and Simpson backs, a strong half-back line of Kindersley, Seddon and Mack, and a forward line of Huddy, Ashby, Boyle, Diplock and Lancelot Pares. The defence was secure enough to keep out all Woolston's attacks, and to everyone's huge satisfaction the home side won by the only goal, scored in the second half by Ashby.

At the party in the Blue Anchor afterwards the cup was presented by General Harward, Vice-President of the club. He made an appropriate speech mentioning many of the players by name, and of course gave the game away by referring to Smith throughout as Doyle. He concluded, neatly enough, by remarking that football was:

> "a manly pastime demanding skill and physical training. Men fond of such sports made good soldiers in the field".

(Lots of "Hear, hears"). Toasts, songs, and general jollification followed until a late hour. General Harward at least did not have far to go home; his house was the first one on Kingston Crescent, just across the road from the pub (it was pulled down in the 1970s, but its imposing pillared doorcase is said to be still fronting a house in St Thomas's Street). One wonders if, on his way back down Fratton Road and over the railway bridge to Elm Grove, Dr Doyle pondered on the contrast between this evening of open-hearted merriment and his weird, hand holding sessions — all in the interests of Science, of course — round the table in General Drayson's darkened sitting-room.

He didn't forget the name, anyway; for, as Holmes remarks in *The Retired Colourman*:

> "With your natural advantages, Watson, every lady is your helper and accomplice... I can picture you whispering sweet nothings with the young lady at the Blue Anchor, and receiving hard somethings in exchange".

It says something for Dr Doyle's personality that, although not yet thirty and a civilian, he found himself perfectly at home in the company of these senior Army officers, and they in his. A fighter himself, he was always interested in history and battles and probably ready enough to lend an ear to some of their reminiscences. He does not seem to have had so much to do with the Royal Navy — though he did later provide a Gunnery trophy for the Channel Fleet. Naval officers — perhaps wedded too strictly to the traditions of the Silent Service — did not feature largely in the affairs of the Literary Society. A Captain Jackson of the Dockyard was a member, but he never spoke.

On the day of the Cup match the *Portsmouth Times* printed a letter from General Harward inviting support for his proposal to provide a Working Mens' Jubilee Memorial to the Queen. This was Victoria's Golden Jubilee year. There was to be a grand Fleet Review at Spithead, and the Town Council had already met to consider other ways and means of marking the celebrations; money was to be allocated for improvements to the Board Schools, playing fields and similar projects. General Harward however thought that something having a more personal connection with Her Majesty should be included; and if the money to provide it could be found from a special collection, just a penny or two each maybe, from all working men in the town, it would more directly demonstrate everyone's loyalty and affection for the Great Lady herself.

Dr Doyle had no doubt about his own feelings for the Queen, and immediately wrote in support:

> "...A Sovereign whose conduct of affairs may serve as a model to every future occupant of the British Throne. It is no exaggeration to say that since the days of Edward the Confessor no English monarch has ever led so consistently virtuous a life or has ever had so beneficient an influence upon the domestic lives and social habits of her subjects...A small personal memorial to the Queen, in the shape of a bust or statue... In conclusion, I may suggest that the statue might adorn the new Town Hall".

On the following Friday, having failed to win over the Council, the two sponsors held a meeting to consider the General's proposal, and decided to try and carry out their scheme by private efforts, namely "to erect a pedestal, with a suitable inscription and possibly a bust of the Queen, near the Town Hall".

The hard weather of winter and early spring did not prevent the Literary Society from completing a full season of six more meetings. The Reverend H. Shaen Solly of Southampton presented a long history of mediaeval Miracle Plays; and in *The Sign Of Four* we duly find that Sherlock Holmes is able to discuss the subject of Miracle Plays as if he had made a special study of them. Dr Mumby, Medical Officer of Health, spoke on The Air We Breathe, listing the diseases which could arise from impure air, bad ventilation and poor sanitation — they were down in the drains again. This led Dr Claremont to observe that people should understand that the night air was not deleterious, and that they should sleep with their bedroom windows open. Another new

speaker was Hugh MacLaughlan, the Editor of the *Evening News,* and
he actually chose a literary subject for his paper, the Poets and Writers
of Elizabethan times. Dr Doyle rose to propose the vote of thanks.
Acting the part of the Plain Man in a topic which did interest him
considerably, he remarked how the Elizabethan period was the time
when the country was in its lusty boyhood, and at the same time the
most musical nation in Europe. The first blow to this character was
struck when Cromwell's troops struck down the Maypoles, but:

> "by far the greatest blow fell when it became fashionable to graft
> on to a stout healthy language the terms and phrases of dead
> languages — to call children Elizabethia and Sophonista instead of
> Polly or Mary..."

At the end-of-season meeting in April the Council of the Society
took the trouble to record in the minutes:

> "its great satisfaction at the appointment of Dr Conan Doyle as
> additional Honorary Secretary, and its appreciation of his valuable
> services during the past year, and of the active part he has always
> taken in the proceedings of the Society".

The Council also took note of two revolutionary proposals. For some
time it had been apparent that while the lectures usually managed to
attract gratifyingly large audiences, most of the listeners were guests,
particularly ladies, and the actual membership numbers remained
pretty static at around one hundred. Already this season 22 members
had moved out of the district, and a further four had been "removed
by death", to quote the secretaries' favourite phrase. Mr Alexander
Howell offered two suggestions to remedy this state of affairs: that the
subscription be reduced to half a guinea, and that ladies be admitted
to membership.

The Council was properly cautious on this one. Dr Doyle said that
he himself entirely agreed with the admission of ladies, but the
meeting generally felt that such an important decision was not one to
be taken rashly by themselves alone, and that the general body of
members should be consulted first. They thus happily put off deciding
anything until the annual meeting the following year. The Editor of the
Hampshire Post, however, in reporting this meeting, had to have his bit
of fun. Referring to the fact that if elected, ladies would naturally be
required to pay their own subscription, he quipped:

> "Whether the ladies will care to be taxed in this way, for the bare
> recognition of their equality with men, when they know very well,
> without any payment at all, that they are greatly superior, remains
> to be seen. But, since they are admitted with gentlemen to witness
> the performances, there is no reason why they should not be asked,

the same as in the case of gentlemen, to pay for the privilege. The subscription will of course confer upon them the right of participating in discussions, but we sincerely trust that they will refrain. . ."

In the world outside the comfortable square mile of Southsea, life's problems continued to arise with depressing regularity. From the *Evening News*, a couple of "casualties":

23 February (a freezing cold day):
"John Broadwood, a lad, pleaded guilty to a charge of begging in the square at Titchfield. Prisoner said he belonged to Maidstone and was searching for work. He expressed his willingness to join the Navy, and Mr Kinshott undertook to take him to the Naval Recruiting Office at Portsmouth tomorrow".

Hunger replaces the Press Gang?

26 February:
"Terrible Fatality in Portsmouth Dockyard. Walter Weekes, aged 26, a skilled labourer, was in the act of putting a strap on the wheel in the grindstone department when he became entangled in the machinery, and was with terrible velocity swept around the shaft. . . On his being extricated it was found that he had sustained a compound fracture of the skull (his brains being dashed all over the workshop); the right arm was torn from his body, both ankles were fractured, and the body was otherwise badly mutilated. The remains were taken to the Dockyard Surgery and seen by Dr Sedgewick".

And from the *Portsmouth Times*, something which I thought only ever happened in Grand Opera:

18 May:
"Romantic Suicide. Two young Munich ladies, the Baronesses Anna and Louise Guttenberg, age 26 and 23, committed suicide by drowning themselves in the Starnberg Lake, on the identical spot where the King of Bavaria was found dead eleven months ago. They had held many melancholy conversations on the tragical fate of the monarch, and repeatedly went to the lake merely to throw flowers on to the watery grave. At last they gave way to the impulse of following the King's example and, taking a boat, rowed to the spot, which is close to the shore, and dropped silently into the water. Next morning. . . they were found in the soft clay firmly clasped in each other's arms. They were both pretty, highly cultivated and rich".

From the same paper, a sad case of a different kind:

20 July:

"Heartless indifference. On Friday the Birmingham Borough Coroner held an inquest on the body of William Joseph Hobson, aged 9. While playing by the side of the canal deceased fell into the water. His companions told three men what had happened, and one of them said "I don't care", another said "Let him stop in", and the third "I ain't got any time to fetch him out". The body was not recovered until the next day. A verdict of accidentally drowned was recorded".

The hard winter had been followed by a good summer (it doesn't always happen). The sun came out, the grass dried, the elms spread shady arms over the Grove, and by early May the cricketers were all out airing their flannels. Portsmouth had a full list of fixtures with local sides, and entered for the Hampshire County Challenge Cup. They fielded a varied side, having several talented newcomers available to back up the regulars Doyle, Hayter, and Hemingsley. J.H. Smith from the Grammar School, a high-scoring batsman and useful slow right arm bowler, was again prominent. The final tally was 11 matches won out of 19 played, 3 drawn and 5 lost. They got as far as the semi-final of the Cup, but then lost to an Ordnance Survey team from Southampton on a day when they were not at full strength.

A.C. Smith featured regularly as opening batsman. In the early games he scored 19 against the Grammar School, 16 against Ryde, 21 in a Cup match, and 23 against Havant, several times being partnered by the other Smith. What's that again? A.C. Smith? Has Dr Doyle now reverted to his football alias for cricket as well? It would seem so, but then, half way through July, the score sheets show him under his proper name once more. Perhaps it was no more than a mental aberration, coming on top of the football season, though whether on the part of the doctor himself or the *Portsmouth Times* reporter it is impossible to say. In the batting averages he came fourth with an average of 15.6 from 18 innings, and was described as "the most consistent scorer, always exhibiting stubborn defence". J.H., the real Smith, was top with 43.3 from 13 innings. In bowling Dr Doyle came seventh, just below Hemingsley, with 16 wickets for an average of 13.1 runs each.

A match against HMS Excellent, the Royal Navy Gunnery Training ship, had a very surprising outcome. Portsmouth won the toss and went in first. They made a bad start, losing 4 wickets for only 13 runs, but managed to put together a total of 105. Excellent then went in, and had scored 66 for 4 when, says the *Portsmouth Times*:

"they suspended the game in a most extraordinary manner. Carnell was thrown out, but instead of accepting the decision, abused the Portsmouth umpire (Mr J. Shaw), and induced his side not to go on with the innings. Portsmouth remained in the field for the necessary interval, then claimed the match on stumps being drawn. It should be added that Mr Shaw has acted as umpire for nearly 35 years... Several independent onlookers were of opinion his decision was correct... Excellent's proper course, instead of shouting at him in discourteous terms and declining to play out the match, was to have protested against his continuing to act as umpire".

Abusing the umpire indeed; who said that was just a late twentieth century practice? Dr Doyle, who always believed that a game was there to be won, would as Captain have had no hesitation in sticking to the letter of the law and claiming as victory a match which his side had looked set to lose. One cannot help wondering what Queen Victoria, let alone the Captain of HMS Excellent, may have felt if this incident had been brought to her attention. Discourteous behaviour on the cricket field? By our Royal Navy? And our Gunnery School, of all places, the home of Naval etiquette and drill? We should certainly not have been amused by that one.

One pleasant little occasion when Her Majesty was amused may perhaps be related here, taken from the *Portsmouth Times* of 6 July:

"Six Scotch bailies came up to town to present an address of congratulations to Her Majesty. They asked what they had to do on entering the Queen's presence, and were told they should kiss hands. Thereupon Bailie No 1, as he solemnly stalked past the throne, raised his hand to his mouth and blew Her Majesty a kiss. The remaining five followed suit, till the Queen had a fit of the heartiest laughter she has enjoyed for a long time".

Saturday 23 July was the day of the great Jubilee Review of the Fleet, and the papers were filled with sketches of the anchorage and of individual ships, and full-page accounts of the scene as viewed from Portsmouth, Gosport and the Isle of Wight. The Royal Navy assembled no fewer than 109 ships, 34 of them battleships or cruisers, in four impressive columns extending from Southsea Castle to Stokes Bay, ready for the Queen to inspect them from the Royal Yacht. The assembly was not carried out without mishap. HMS Devastation had been designated the leading ship of one column but was delayed getting away from her anchorage at Portland. Her Captain put on extra speed to overhaul the others, and having succeeded in doing so, turned his ship to starboard to take up his proper station. Unfortunately he miscalculated his manoeuvre and crossed the bows of the next ship in line, HMS Ajax, too soon, with the result that Ajax's bow rammed him in the starboard quarter. Damage to Ajax was slight; Devastation was holed and one compartment flooded, but both ships were able to complete the passage under their own power. Luckily there were no casualties, except no doubt for Captain Luxmore himself, who must have seen his hopes of crowning his career with an Admiral's flag vanish in that moment, and spent the Review period wondering how he was now going to be able to manage on his Captain's pension.

There is no record of whether Conan Doyle visited any of the ships or attended any of the receptions, but he and Louise would certainly have walked down to Southsea front, like everyone else, and viewed with pride the armada from the Esplanade or the Castle ramparts. As it happened, he was at that time engaged in another newspaper argument. The cause at issue was vaccination — the familiar technique pioneered by Jenner and Pasteur in which protection against contagious disease is obtained by inoculating the subject with a minute dose of the disease itself. At that time it was compulsory to vaccinate all new babies in Britain against smallpox; Parliament had directed that it should be carried out before the age of three months, and laid down a standard fee of threepence. It was another of the family doctor's regular chores. Nevertheless there was considerable opposition in many places. On 14 July the *Portsmouth Evening Mail* (a rival paper of the *Evening News*) published a letter from a retired Lieutenant-Colonel A.T. Wintle, of 6 South Parade, condemning the practice on the grounds that it was immoral, it did not work, and only led to an increased risk of passing on other infections. Dr Doyle immediately seized his pen and wrote a forceful reply, quoting statistics to prove his case. Colonel Wintle wrote again, and the argument spread to the *Portsmouth Times*. In his letter to that paper, published on 27 July, Dr Doyle, in clear, positive and downright language, demolished the anti-vaccination case point by point. He went on:

> "Only the possession of an extremely strong case can justify a man in opposing medical men upon a medical point, and this is of all the points the one which should be most cautiously approached, as the welfare of the whole community is at stake. Should I put forward some positive and dogmatic views upon the rifling of guns or the the trajectory of a shell, Colonel Wintle, as an artillerist, would be justified in demanding that I should produce some good reasons for the faith that was in me. The tendency of the scientific work not only of Pasteur and of Koch, but also of Burdon-Sanderson, Toussaint and others, lies more and more in the direction of protective methods of inoculation to check zymotic disease...
>
> Yours faithfully,
>
> A. Conan Doyle MD CM".

Whether any other of the dozens of doctors in Portsmouth had thought of replying to Colonel Wintle, we do not know. Dr Doyle was in any case not the man to wait on someone else's decision, and after his reply they must have felt that no other was needed. We will forgive him his little piece of medical one-upmanship; by zymotic he just means infectious.

It may have been about this time that Dr Doyle began his diversification into eye specialisation. There is no record of the exact date; he simply states, referring in his autobiography to the year 1890:

"Of late years I had been interested in eye work and had amused myself by correcting refractions and ordering glasses in the Portsmouth Eye Hospital under Mr Vernon Ford".

Quite possibly he had a genuine interest in this particular aspect of medicine. It may even have been George Budd at Plymouth who first put the idea into his head, if the words he put into this doctor's mouth in *The Stark Munro Letters* had a foundation in fact:

"I've taken to the eye, my boy. There's a fortune in the eye. A man grudges a half-crown to cure his chest or his throat, but he'd spend his last dollar over his eye. There's money in ears, but the eye is a gold mine".

Certainly it would offer an additional outlet, a means of augmenting the routine work of his general practice, without going to the trouble and expense of getting a specialist qualification in surgery. It could mean more money, too. A bill to Mr Chapman dated 26 November 1890 — one of the last he had to present in Southsea — and inscribed "To testing child's eyes etc. 5/- " suggests that he could charge a little more than his routine half-crown or three and sixpence for this more specialised attention. The difference looks trivial now, but in terms of Victorian money, and multiplied up over a year, it could be significant enough in a practice still making only about £300.

The Portsmouth Eye Hospital was almost a Ford family concern. The driving spirit behind its creation was the father of the family, Richard William Ford, a solicitor of St Thomas's Street, Old Portsmouth; a prominent citizen, one-time Mayor, and Clerk of the peace for many years. It was he who convened the original meeting in August 1884 to consider the establishment of a small hospital which could take eye and ear cases away from the Royal, and it was largely due to his efforts that sufficient money was raised to render the project practicable. He remained Chairman of the Hospital Committee until his death in 1900. He had a large family, and the five survivors of his seven sons all made successful careers in the professions. Two became lawyers, one an architect. Arthur Vernon Ford, born in 1854, was the ophthalmic surgeon. The youngest, Richard William born in 1857, reached General rank in the Royal Army Medical Corps and was knighted.

The hospital was opened on 1 December 1884 in the end house of an old terrace in Pembroke Road called Clarence View. It started with just five rooms and three beds. Dr Ward Cousins and Dr Vernon Ford were its two medical officers, and there was one nurse. In its first year they treated no fewer than 1600 patients. Gradually it became possible to expand, but as with all these voluntary institutions there was a constant struggle to raise enough funds to keep it going. Vernon Ford's wife Margaret took a leading part in many of these activities; the children's fancy dress ball which she organised every Christmas quickly became a notable fixture in the social life of the town. By 1887 they were treating over 2000 cases a year, and it is pretty evident that Dr Doyle's services, once he had mastered the routine non-surgical work, would be a valuable addition. As a sportsman himself with a particularly good eye, as well as a humanitarian, he may well have felt a special sympathy towards the younger patients — more than a quarter of the total were under ten years old — quite apart from any value the experience afforded to himself, and he maintained his connection with the Eye Hospital to the end of his time in Portsmouth.

Meanwhile, as if all this were not enough, he was thinking about his next book. He cannot have been particularly cheered up to notice that in July the *Portsmouth Times* began a weekly serialisation of *Herr Paulus: his Rise, his Greatness, and his Fall*, the latest novel of Portsmouth author Walter Besant, while his own *The Firm Of Girdlestone & Co* and *Study in Scarlet* still lay practically unread. Walter Besant, a heavily bearded, bespectacled figure, was a writer highly thought of in his time and has a street named after him in Fratton. Some of his novels provide interesting glimpses of life in Portsmouth in the early years of the century, but nobody has time to read them now. He gets a brief mention, by name only, in a delightful short story by Conan Doyle called *Cyprian Overbeck Wells (A Literary Mosaic)* which came out in the Christmas number of the *Boy's Own Paper* in 1886, and in which he poked good-natured fun at some of Britain's literary giants, and more particularly at himself. Writing as usual in the first person, he cast himself as a young man with the ambition to write a great novel but with no idea how to go about it. He even gave himself his footballing alias of Smith. Seated one evening after supper with the blank sheets in front of him:

"in that comfortable lethargic condition which accompanies both digestion and poisoning by nicotine"

he dreams that he is surrounded by a dozen of these famous writers — Defoe, Smollett, Scott, Swift, Dickens and others, plus a contemporary or two, not forgetting Walter Besant. They start a story among themselves, passing the tale from one to another in turn (a Literary Mosaic), and Conan Doyle cleverly mimics the style and expression of each. The Editor of the *Boy's Own Paper* deserves our respect for accepting this little tour-de-force — even if its subtleties may have been lost on some of his readers. (Interestingly enough, the 2 July issue of *Light* contained a reference to *Herr Paulus, his Rise, his Greatness, his Fall*, which it said "deals with certain aspects of modern Spiritualism").

However, having got his detective story out of the way, Dr Doyle had now conceived the ambition to write a historical novel. The notion had obviously been boiling up inside him for some time. His enthusiasm for it comes across strongly in *Memories and Adventures*, in contrast to the passing reference to his eye work:

> "Feeling large thoughts rise within me, I now determined to test my powers to the full".

This was going to be no half-length effort like *Study In Scarlet* but a full-scale, 500-page job. The actual labour of writing didn't deter him one whit; if Sir Walter Scott could knock off a Waverley novel in three months — writing by candlelight, with a scratchy dip pen, and carrying on a legal practice at the same time - well, so could he. What he wanted to get on to the page was adventure, movement, battles, fights, a touch of romance maybe (but not enough to get in the way), but mostly fights and the winning of them. Schoolboy stuff, perhaps? Well, partly. His own self-confessed readership was "the boy who's half a man, and the man who's half a boy", but the backcloth would still be authentic English history. During the autumn he would read up Macaulay and any other authorities he could find on the Monmouth rebellion; then, in the long winter evenings his young hero Micah Clarke would come to life on the pages.

Some of the long evenings, anyway. There was still the Literary Society to think of; its fortnightly meetings were much too big a part of the social scene to be neglected. On Friday 21 October, after a day of energetic dusting and polishing, Louise welcomed the gentlemen of the Society's Council to her modest front room for their pre-season meeting. Drs Claremont and Guillebard, Percy Boulnois, MacLaughlan of the *News* and three or four others were there, besides Dr Cousins and her husband. Did they spend all evening on their deliberations over sherry and cigars, or adjourn to the Bush afterwards for a quick one before going home? Bush Villa may not have been as grand a house as some, but its location certainly had its advantages.

The Society was flourishing. Cogswell the architect had joined this year. So had Lysander Maybury, the police surgeon. So also had at least one important member of the Town Council. Mr A.W. White was manager of the Provincial Tramway Company; and from his offices at

Cambridge Junction he also ran one of the town's largest furniture removal and general carriage businesses, a firm which still carries his name today. He had been a prominent citizen for many years, and it may be due to his influence that, early in the following year, the Society was offered the use of a room in the Guildhall for its meetings and so was able to escape from the draughty and dusty confines of the Penny Street Lecture Hall. He was also Chairman of the Portsmouth Liberal-Unionist Association, and Dr Doyle was his Vice-Chairman.

Hugh MacLaughlan led off the lecture season with a piece on the history of the Old Portsmouth Theatre, not forgetting of course to include a mention of its connection with Mr Vincent Crummles's Travelling Company in Dickens's *Nicholas Nickleby*. A Dr George Smith gave an account of his three years' residence as a medical officer in the Congo, and therby gave Dr Doyle the chance to say something of his own brief visit to West Africa. The doctors really came into their own at the meeting on 20 December when Dr Claremont read a learned paper entitled "Our Knowledge of Brain", for the discussion quickly turned on to the new and then fashionable fringe science of Phrenology. The medical establishment, as we might expect, were with one exception all against it. Dr Cousins said that the doctrines were not worth the paper they were written on; phrenology was "the baseless fabric of a vision". General Drayson, the polymath, got up to object. He had had 1500 students and 400 officers pass through his hands, he said, all of whom he had noticed phrenologically. He considered he was able to tell if a scholar were well adapted for a course of study, and if he would be quick at application. He drew a diagram on the board to illustrate his point, but was at once shot down by Dr Cousins, who told him that all he had drawn was a skull, which was nothing to do with the point at issue. It was Dr Doyle, however, who, eager as ever to know more, said that he would be glad if any gentleman in the room would at some future meeting take up the case for phrenology.

The other winter activities and events followed in their turn. Messrs Cadburys advertised that fourteen breakfast cups of strong, reliable Cocoa could be made from a sixpenny packet of cocoa essence; "Ask for CADBURYS and do not be imposed upon". A Mr John Ley, 45, of 29 Grosvenor Street, was fined 20 shillings for being drunk in charge of a horse. An inquest was held on Annie Tee, aged 16, who had been found dead in her bed in a miserable lodging-house near the Dockyard. Born illegitimate, she had been boarded out by her mother at the age of nine months, and was on the streets of Portsea by the time she was fourteen. Death was due to pleurisy, both lungs being badly congested. The November gales came in dead on time at the beginning of the month. Chimneys were blown off, windows shattered, the Isle of Wight ferries and even the Floating Bridge across the harbour were halted. At high tide the water was eighteen inches deep half way up Broad Street, and the sea overflowed into the moat of Southsea Castle.

Dr Doyle played in goal against the Royal Scots Greys when Portsmouth won by three goals to nil, but had to miss a couple of early games. The annual meeting of the Club was held at the Albany on 15 September, when it was stated that for the previous season they had the best record of any club in the whole of Hampshire and Dorset. General Sir George Willis, GOC Southern District, was elected President for the coming year. Besides Dr Conan Doyle the list of Vice-Presidents included the town's two Members of Parliament, three more Generals and an Admiral, thereby initiating a long tradition of Service links with the Pompey club. F.J. Seddon, a clever and powerful half-back, was to be the new Captain.

On 5 November, Guy Fawkes night, nearly three hundred persons took part in the annual demonstration and march by the Orange Lodge of Portsmouth, led by the Reverend H.Lindsay Young. At a rally in the Albert Hall, Commercial Road afterwards he made a long and virulently anti-Catholic speech. It was not true, he said, that an Orangeman was one who had taken an oath to wade knee-deep in Catholic blood. It was not true that the Orange Lodge was a political organisation, but the only safeguard against the ever-present threat of Papist domination was eternal vigilance. We had heard far too much already of the Godless cry of Home Rule, he thundered, waving his fist in the air, and so on, in language which we are only too familiar with today, a hundred years on.

The Mighty Fine, Commercial Road, Portsmouth. Formerly called the Albany Hotel. this became the headquarters of both Portsmouth Football Club and Portsmouth Cricket Club in the late 1880s, when Dr Conan Doyle was a member of them.

(Photo: R.F. Reynolds, Cosham).

Luckily for him, perhaps, Dr Doyle was not present at that event. Nor was he at the annual muncipal banquet in the Victoria Hall on 9 November. Plenty of familiar names were there — Dr Knott, Dr Maybury, Arthur Cogswell, John Brickwood, Percy Boulnois, Richard Ford, the Mayor and all the high-ups on the Town Council. But he did find himself invited, along with several other Literary Society colleagues including Dr Watson, on to the Mayor's Committee to consider the arrangements for the forthcoming banquet in honour of Walter Besant. He and Louise were not listed among those attending a ball at Sandringham House which had been got up by a group of sporting gentlemen styling themselves the Zodiacs, of whom Dr Vernon Ford was one. They may well, however, have been among the audience at a thought-reading entertainment presented by Le Chevalier Cumberland at the Portland Hall on 30 November:

> "A gentleman on the platform was requested to think of a lady to whom he would like that a bouquet should be presented. The gentleman having thought, the Chevalier, blindfolded, led him to the lady who had been selected".

Dr Doyle himself may not have been present at Mr Godfrey's two piano recitals given by the young prodigy Josef Hoffman; nor was he listed among the Brethren attending the annual meeting of Phoenix Lodge on 29 December, but he did attend the dinner and smoking concert of the Bowling Club at the Bush, there to propose the toast of "The Press" and also to receive his prize, "two volumes of a valuable surgical work". And on 8 December he was in London, representing Portsmouth at a conference of Liberal-Unionists in Westminster Town Hall, where he presented Lord Hartington, the President, with an address of support signed by A.W. White and himself.

His proudest moment, however, must have come at some time after the middle of November, when there appeared on the bookstalls the highly coloured cover of a soft-backed booklet bearing the heading *Beeton's Christmas Annual*, and underneath in large red letters A STUDY IN SCARLET. The author's name, plain A. Conan Doyle, was printed in black, plus, in much smaller lettering, the titles of the other contents of the Annual, two original Drawing Room Plays. After a period of gestation of eighteen months, Sherlock Holmes had finally been born.

Everyone has heard of Mrs Beeton, whose famous book of Household Management ("to prepare the sauce, take a dozen eggs. . .") came out in 1856. Mr Beeton, her husband, had been a director of Ward, Lock and Company, and so immortalised his own name through the cover of this Annual. According to *The Crescent*, a Portsmouth magazine of the period, the Annual was sold out within a fortnight. As is the way with such ephemera, most copies, having passed through the hands of the family, were consigned by tidy housewives to the dustbin, or perhaps used up in lighting the kitchen fire, and the few copies which do remain are very jealously guarded. The book aroused little interest nationally, and singularly little among most of the Portsmouth Papers, notwithstanding its local author. The *Hampshire Telegraph*, which included a four-page literary section every week, had columns

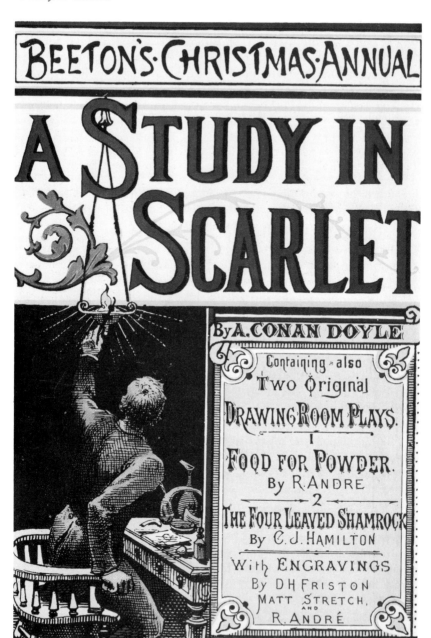

The cover of *Beeton's Christmas Annual* for 1887, in which Sherlock Holmes made his first appearance in print.

Part of a page from *The Bookseller* dated 5 November, 1887, advertising "A Study in Scarlet", the first Sherlock Holmes story.

of space devoted to short reviews of all the latest publications. The issue of 3 December contained a note on the Christmas number of the *Boy's Own Paper*, which included among its contents:

"an exceedingly well written sketch of life in the diamond mines, entitled *The Stone of Boxman's Drift*, by Dr Conan Doyle, who also contributes an epic of the late Egyptian campaign entitled *Corporal Dick's Promotion*",

but it failed completely to notice *Beeton's*. The *Portsmouth Times*, which carried fewer reviews than the *Telegraph*, was equally unobservant, as was the *Evening News*. Sherlock Holmes's entry into the world had been as stealthy as some of his own investigations, but not entirely unnoticed. Dr Doyle, of course, would not want to puff his own book too obviously, but there was no reason why a loyal wife like Louise should not tell their friends about it, and the news would quickly get around the literary and medical circles of Southsea. It was left to that observant and highly literate writer, the Editor of the *Hampshire Post*, however, to draw the attention of the Portsmouth public at large to the new phenomenon in their midst. The *Post* was an eight-page broadsheet very similar in appearance and content to the *Portsmouth Times* and *Hampshire Telegraph*. It came out once a week on Fridays and was published by Messrs Mills and Sons, of Palmerston Road, who also operated a bookshop and a circulating library. On 2 December it carried a first leader, one and a half columns in length, boldly headed A STUDY IN SCARLET, and comprising a most thorough review of the whole story, containing as much enthusiastic praise and at the same time valid criticism as any new author could wish for. The article began:

> "Under this title Dr A. Conan Doyle, one of the Honorary Secretaries of our local Literary and Scientific Society, has composed a Christmas Annual which is certain to attract a host of readers... We still have bloody tragedies in plenty related for our Christmas enjoyment, but homicide is now combined with the achievements of the Detective. By these means the mind of the reader is enthralled by a two-fold charm. His interest is excited by the circumstances of the atrocity and the events leading up to it, and his attention is afterwards absorbed in following the marvellous steps by which the detective Nemesis pursues the murderer with the sure instinct of a sleuth hound. Of breathless recitals of this character we know of no more brilliant example than the little story which Dr Doyle has just given to the world..."

Sherlock Holmes's qualities are properly appreciated:

> "His detective is a marvellous creation, and the study of him which is given at the beginning is one of the most carefully elaborated portions of the book. As a painstaking delineation of abnormal activity HOLMES is far ahead of the heroes of Gaboriau and Borisgobey..."

The article compares *A Study In Scarlet* favourably with the mystery tales of Gaboriau, Poe and Wilkie Collins, but does not overlook the weak points in its construction. With regard to the long central section on the Mormons (in which Holmes does not appear), the Editor remarks:

> "This subsidiary thread is remarkably well written and intensely exciting... Here we lose the acquaintance of JOHN WATSON MD, who is supposed to relate the story, and are indebted to the pen of the impersonal historian for a knowledge of what may be regarded as the motive of the crime... but we see no reason why Dr Watson

should not have been made to narrate the FERRIER episode from 'information received' from the prisoner. . ."

He notes Jefferson Hope's apparently motiveless stupidty in going back to the scene of the murder to recover the victim's wedding ring:

"Verily, it is not so much the sagacity of detectives as the stupidity of the criminal classes which bring offenders to their doom".

And concludes reasonably:

". . .it is to be remembered that, notwithstanding all the amazing powers, cleverness and acquirements of Sherlock Holmes, the detection of the murderer was owing almost exclusively to the exercise of sound commonsense, an ingredient which is of far more importance in a detective than those phenomenal qualities with which the novelist is apt to endow his creations".

If Dr Doyle did not already have the *Hampshire Post* delivered to his door every Friday, we should be surprised if he did not change his order after this particular issue.

CHAPTER VII

1888 - His Best Work Is Quite Good

ON THE EVENING of Tuesday 31 January Mr A.W. Jerrard rose to address the Literary Society, now meeting in the the Town Hall, or rather the Guildhall as it was becoming customary to call it. His appearance on the platform was something of an event in itself. A tall, portly figure, clean-shaven except for a set of bushy side-whiskers which emphasised his magisterial appearance, he was the Headmaster of Portsmouth Grammar School. Not yet forty, unmarried, dedicated to his job, he had been appointed in 1878 when the school was almost non-existent and had already succeeded in building up its population to just under 400; but although he had been a member of the Society for nearly ten years this was the first time he had ever taken any active part in the proceedings.

He had got a first in History at Oxford, and his subject this evening was the Irish politician and novelist Justin McCarthy — a man known in his time as a genial satirist but who had recently made another name for himself by publishing a popular history of the first forty years of Queen Victoria's reign. Mr Jerrard's paper, long and learned as it was, is of more interest to us for the exchanges it led to afterwards. After a few words from the proposer, Dr Doyle rose to second the vote of thanks. He paid a warm tribute to the speaker and his subject, then went on to say that in his estimation there was never a period when contemporary fiction was at such low ebb. True, we had such figures as Walter Besant and James Payn (Editor of *The Cornhill*), but even these, he felt, would confirm that there was no one to equal the stature of Dickens or Thackeray, or even such lower lights as George Eliot or Charles Reade. And unfortunately, he added with becoming modesty, he saw no prospect of any revival in the near future.

Mr Jerrard, in reply, especially thanked Dr Conan Doyle for the compliment he had paid him. The novel which had "created such a sensation at the close of the year", entitled *A Study in Scarlet*, which he had no doubt they had all read (applause) entitled Dr Conan Doyle to express the opinions which he had, and justified them all in hoping that he himself might prove to be a star in the literary firmament (renewed applause).

The "sensation" which Mr Jerrard referred to was presumably only a local one. True, the little paperback had been favourably noticed by other newspapers up and down the country: the *Bristol Mercury*, the *Birmingham Post*, the *Glasgow Herald*, the *Scotsman*. The last-named even went so far as to say "the author shows genius". Mr Jerrard is hardly likely to have been aware of these. Indeed, the author himself may not have been. If his publisher had told him of them, Dr Doyle may have received the information with rather mixed feelings. At about this time the papers were beginning to print occasional paragraphs praising another detective tale, *The Mystery of a Hansom Cab*, by an Australian, Fergus W. Hume. These were in fact thinly disguised advertisements puffing the book's sales, which by the end of May were said to have reached no fewer than 372,869 copies in five months. Dr Doyle's sympathies, though he thought the tale itself was weak, must all have been with that author who, like himself, had been compelled to sell the copyright outright and never received more than his flat fee of £50. All the same, it must have brought a flush of pride and gratification to his cheeks to receive such a fulsome tribute from a senior academic, in front of his home audience; even if, by now, Sherlock Holmes had been banished to the past while his head was teeming with all the facts he wanted to get on to paper about his new hero Micah Clarke.

Subject, as always, to his other commitments. There was the practice, for a start. Although there must have been times quite often when, like Watson's, his practice was not very absorbing, it was still his bread-and-butter and was likely to be busy enough in the cold months.

There were social engagements, too. The civic banquet for Walter Besant was held on 19 January. Over four hundred gentlemen and their ladies sat down in the Victoria Hall, headed by the Mayor and Corporation, local Members of Parliament and senior officers of the Army and Navy. Dr and Mrs Doyle were included, at one guinea for the double ticket. It was by far the grandest function to which Louise had been taken by her husband. In her best dress (a new one, we hope), she would have been much interested in what all the great ladies of the town were wearing. Dr Doyle, handing her out of their hired cab, would have been more conscious of how many of his friends and colleagues were driven up in their own carriages, and wondered what he had to do next to achieve that standard of affluence for himself. Louise would have felt even grander if her husband had been invited to propose one of the many toasts, but he was still too far down in the civic pecking order for that privilege here.

A much lighter engagement was the annual meeting of the Portsmouth Cricket Club, held not at the Blue Anchor but at the Albany Hotel on 25 January, at which Dr Doyle was re-elected Captain. And there was the extraordinary drawn-out saga of the Portsmouth and District Football Challenge Cup, in which both semi-finals and also the final had all to be played no fewer than three times.

Portsmouth, having already drawn their semi-final against Hilsea Ramblers twice, met them again at the Officers Ground on 7 January. They were missing the services of Norman Pares (who was in the Grammar School cup team and therefore ineligible), but had A.C. Smith at right back, A.H. Wood at inside right, and another sporting clergyman, the Reverend A.W. Plant, curate of St Michael's church Landport, at inside left. Both sides scored, but Portsmouth's goal was disputed. It was upheld by both "umpires" (linesmen), but the referee overruled them, disallowed the goal, and awarded the match to Hilsea. Portsmouth gave notice to lodge a protest.

In the other semi-final Portsmouth Grammar School drew twice with Havant but managed to win the second replay. So the final, or rather the first version of it, took place on 18 February, a bitterly cold day, between the School and Hilsea Ramblers. Hilsea won by the only goal, but now it was the School's turn to protest; one of Hilsea's men was ineligible, they alleged. The Cup Committee duly met to consider the two complaints, and upheld them both. Hilsea were disqualified and a new final was played on 17 March, between Portsmouth and the Grammar School. It was another freezing day, with a cutting north wind and flurries of snow. The School had Norman Pares at back and J.H. Smith at centre forward, while A.C. Smith was once more in goal for Portsmouth. Both teams were said to be in capital form, but all the attacks of the School were foiled by the powerful defence of the home team:

> "the latter being especially indebted to their goalkeeper, who saved point after point, thanks to his height and reach",

and the result was another draw. A fortnight later they met again, when Portsmouth finally managed to win by three goals to two, thanks to their better weight and staying powers in the second half. So they succeeded in retaining their cup, after all.

The gales and snow of winter continued well into March, throughout Europe as well. It affected some people worse than others. From a paragraph in the *Portsmouth Times* of 21 March:

> "Throwing a Jew to a pack of wolves. A Russian peasant was driving to the market town in his sleigh, carrying for sale a sow and a litter of six young pigs. On the road a poor Jewish journeyman, tramping through the deep snow, besought the peasant's charity to give him a lift... The road lay for some distance through the skirt of a pine wood. The continuous squealing of the litter of pigs, heard at a great distance in the cold and rarefied air, attracted a pack of six or eight wolves. The peasant's horses needed no urging forward, but one after the other the litter was sacrificed to the voracious pursuers. Some little distance remained before the next village, and

the pack was again hard upon the sleigh and its occupants. The Christian peasant considered he had already made a sufficient sacrifice of his property, and in order to save the sow he cast the unfortunate Jew from the sleigh. The wretched man was immediately devoured. The peasant reached the village in safety. He. . . will be formally tried, and possibly condemned to a month's penance in a monastery".

By mid-April the worst of the bad weather was over, but it was to prove to be a disappointing summer. On the 14th the Council of the Literary Society met again at Bush Villa, Dr James Watson among them. They reviewed the past season; Henry Ball had read a paper on architecture, but present-day residents of the town may regret that his broad sweeping treatment left him no room to mention Southsea's own developer, Thomas Owen. Dr Axford was elected President for the next season, and it was confirmed that the question of ladies' membership would be taken up at the forthcoming Annual General Meeting. The *Hampshire Post* reverted to its former line, but in rather more subdued vein:

"We view with some regret the prospective intrusion of the Lady Question at the annual meeting. The alleged desire on the part of ladies to pay a guinea subscription for the express purpose of qualifying themselves to read papers and participate in the subsequent debates, is a fiction. . . there is no evidence that they are carried away by a burning desire to become blue-stockings, and to air their notions in a public arena in the company of gentlemen".

The Annual General Meeting was duly held on 24 April at the Guildhall, when all of sixteen men turned up to represent the membership. After long and tortuous debate the motion "That ladies desirous of joining the Society as Members shall be admitted in the ordinary way" was finally carried "by a large majority" (to quote the minutes), in other words by eight votes to five, three gentlemen abstaining. Now the *Portsmouth Times* decided to have a go. Having Liberal sympathies, it took the opposite line from the Conservative *Hampshire Post*:

". . .judge of our surprise when we learned that five persons, with the outward semblance of humanity, had attempted to deprive Society of this proposed infusion of sweetness and light. The ignoble five. . . have presumably the ordinary machinery of the heart and mind, but the mechanism must be defective; the blood must creep in dribbles through their veins, and the dust of what once was marrow must be mouldering in their bones. . . Come and welcome, lady members of the Portsmouth Literary and Scientific Society! Previous acquaintance with the subjects of discussion is not necessary. Every one of you will carry the marshal's baton in your knapsack, or it would be more accurate to say, the President's hammer in your handbag."

On 17 April, in between these two engagements, Dr Doyle had attended a grand combined Conservative and Liberal-Unionist demonstration at the Amphitheatre in Gunwharf Road. Again, he was not called upon to speak. R.W. Ford, who in addition to his other public appointments was General Chairman of the Portsmouth Conservative Party, presided. The town's two MPs were there, along with others from Hampshire, numbers of retired Admirals and Generals, the Aldermen, Councillors, and other prominent citizens. Lord Cranbrook delivered a long speech which was received with acclaim; and a motion by A.W. White proposing that the status quo in Ireland be maintained was greeted with even louder cheers.

On 27 April Dr Doyle was called upon in his professional capacity to give evidence at a Coroner's inquest held in the Barley Mow, a public house in Castle Road only a few steps from Bush Villa. James Killick, aged 47, a greengrocer, had gone to bed drunk, his usual state. Early in the morning he got up, fell down on the floor and couldn't lift himself up again. His wife ran for help but when she returned with a neighbour they found him apparently lifeless. Dr Doyle was sent for, and confirmed that the man was dead. He gave it as his opinion that death was due to failure of the heart's action, the result of natural causes, and probably brought about by the well-known habits of the deceased.

At the end of the month there was a social occasion of a much happier kind when one of the Reverend Egan Desmond's four daughters was married at St Jude's Church. Dr and Mrs Doyle were not listed among the friends and relations who had sent presents for the bride and bridegroom, but it is impossible to believe that Louise and her mother would have wanted him to miss such a fashionable event happening almost on their doorstep.

All the while, in between times, he was writing, writing, writing. *Micah Clarke* was finally completed, according to Carr, at the end of February; two copies, every word handwritten. It is a long book, a bit wordy in places, especially the early pages, but the action when it gets going is chockfull of incident, adventure and clearly drawn characters. The original title is longwinded, archaic in style and off-putting to a modern reader; "*Micah Clarke His Statement As Made to his Three Grandchildren Joseph, Gervas and Reuben during the hard winter of 1734 wherein is contained a Full Report of Certain Passages in his Early Life. . . etc, Now for the First Time Collected Corrected and Rearranged from the Original Manuscript by A. Conan Doyle*", but it demonstrates how the author again contrived to put himself into the position of first-person narrator —

very much in the way that present-day writers of Sherlockian pastiches (particularly Americans) present themselves as "editors" of newly discovered Watson manuscripts. Critics have complained about the artificial sound of the old-fashioned conversation passages ("Hit the crop-eared rascal over the pate, Jack!"), but there is no holding back the author — or the reader — in the action scenes. The chapter titles are reminiscent in their style of Dickens, but they are indicative of the content: "Of a Passage of Arms at the Blue Boar"; "Of Our Perilous Adventure on the Plain"; "Of Our Brush with the King's Dragoons"; "Of the Fight in Wells Cathedral" and many such more. The theme itself reminds one of Scott's *Waverley*; the young hero Micah finds himself, for perfectly good reasons, embroiled on the wrong side in a rebellious uprising — the son of one of Cromwell's Puritans fighting with the Duke of Monmouth in the attempt to restore a disputed monarchy. Havant and Petersfield, neighbouring villages of Portsmouth (which Dr Doyle had visited often enough with his cricket and football teams) feature in the early episodes; Taunton, the West country and the Battle of Sedgemoor in the later ones. The book is still a good read. School readers, with notes, have been made from it. It was serialised on BBC Radio as recently as April 1985.

Off went the manuscript on the way, like its predecessors, to its first refusal, notwithstanding its author's really high hopes this time. One might have thought that after this great effort he would have taken a break. Perhaps he did, for a weekend or so. But he was already writing to his mother sketching out ideas for further titles, and very soon started on his next opus. For this he went back to the favourite theme of some of his best short stories, and what we may suppose to have been his constant preoccupation at this time: the occult, the supernatural — in this case, as manifested by the religions of the East. By the end of July he had completed a short novel called *The Mystery of Cloomber*. This must be Conan Doyle's least known work. It is not found in second-hand bookshops, it is not referred to by his biographers, and we have to thank the American enthusiasts Gaslight Publications for providing us with a reprint in 1980. Dr Doyle was not particularly pleased with it himself, and it is only too easy to dismiss it as an overblown short story, a pot-boiler, written quickly to fulfill a magazine contract.

The tale concerns a trio of Eastern mystics who come back, from the dead apparently, to exact retribution upon a retired Army officer for a crime committed in India forty years previously. It is admittedly far from perfect in construction, the characters are mostly faceless, the dialogue is flabby, and the action does not really get going until over half way through. The Asians are said to be Buddhist priests of a high order, yet they are seen to be rolling cigarettes (Buddhists do not smoke), they wear red fezes, which makes them Moslems, their leader is called Ram Singh, which makes him a Sikh, the ship's mate calls them niggers, and the narrator speaks of them as "these Hindoos". Indeed, the mix-upfulness is terrific, as another fictional Indian might have said; Conan Doyle was to make the same mistake over his names of the three Asians in *The Sign of Four*, the second Holmes novel. The book has its felicitous touches as well: the first sight of the big house, "The high, white tower of Cloomber Hall, like the headstone of some giant grave"; the prelude to the storm, "A low moaning sound rose up from the ocean as if it knew that trouble was in store for it"; and the aftermath, "All inside the breakers was a seething, gleaming line of foam, as though the fierce old ocean was gnashing its white teeth at the victims who had escaped from its clutches". And the action of the Indian episode, told in flashback, is as vividly done as any of the author's better known battle pieces.

There is a very perfunctory touch of romance, but Conan Doyle's main aim was evidently to leave his readers fascinated but mystified (as he was himself) by the weird powers attributed to the Asian ascetics: the dissociation of the spirit from the body, the ability to foretell and even to influence the future, the facility of communication by thought transference, and even the power of dematerialisation. "This is accomplished", says Ram Singh, "by our power of resolving an object into its chemical atoms, of conveying these atoms with a speed which exceeds that of lightning to any given spot, and of there re-precipitating them and compelling them to retake their original form". This is the TV series *Star Trek's* "Beam us up, Scotty", years before its time! It is a theme which Conan Doyle was to return to — without any deeper foundation in scientific theory — many years later in a Professor Challenger story, *The Disintegration Machine*. To give a sense of authority to his fantasy, he provided a short postscript chapter headed The Occult Philosophy, with quotes from a contemporary work *The Occult World* by A.P. Sinnett.

The Mystery Of Cloomber came out as a serial in two weekly magazines, the *Pall Mall Budget* and the *Pall Mall Gazette* between August and November. In announcing the new serial in its issue of 23 August the Editor of the *Pall Mall Budget* wrote, in his chatty way:

> "We beg to state that next week we shall commence a new story by Doctor DOYLE (a nephew, by the way, of the world-famous 'Dicky'), which he calls 'The Mystery of Cloomber'. When we announced Mr Grant Allen's story some weeks ago we assured our readers that they would find it 'weird and fascinating'. . . 'The Mystery of Cloomber' will be found 'weird and fascinating' too. The scene is laid in the storm-beaten coasts of Scotland. (Don't be frightened; there is no Scotch dialect). The central figure is a haunted General. Who

haunts him, and why he is haunted, will be wrapped in judicious mystery for seven or eight weeks."

Judicious mystery indeed — to the Editor as well, it seems, since one whole chapter of the book is written in Scots dialect.

Meanwhile Messrs Ward, Lock and Company had decided they had a good thing on their hands, and had arranged to publish the principle component of their recent *Beeton's* in book form. This rare volume, the first English edition of *A Study in Scarlet*, came out in July. It carried six shaky pen-and-ink drawings by the author's father, Charles Doyle, and very odd they are, too; Sherlock Holmes is drawn with a full beard, the urchins of the Baker Street Irregulars salute with their left hands, it is Watson who is seen instructing them and not Holmes, and so forth — almost as if the artist, poor man, had not even read his son's book properly. By now, an epileptic and part-time alcoholic, kept apart from his wife and children in a remote Scottish institution, living in an unhappy dream world but not so far gone that he could not still dearly miss his family — might not his figure of Holmes, drawn as it was in his own image, have been a desperate reminder of his own existence, calling out, "Here I am — it is your father, still in being. . . "?

The *Hampshire Post* was not slow to notice the new publication. A paragraph on its leader page of 6 July announced:

> "A STUDY IN SCARLET. This tale (by Dr Conan Doyle of Southsea) which attracted more attention than, perhaps, any of the last Christmas stories, has been re-issued by Ward, Lock and Company. Illustrations have been introduced, and the book is in a light, neat cover. On the story itself we commented at some length at Christmas, and a passage from our remarks has been inserted in this new edition among the 'Opinions of The Press' ".

Two copies of the book, Accession Nos 14,963 and 14,984, were purchased for the Portsmouth Public Library in October. If either of them could be found now, its value might well cover the present library's new book budget for a year.

The author, meanwhile, had been seized with yet another idea. On its leader page of 4 August the *Portsmouth Times* drew the attention of its readers to an article in the current number of a Journal called *The Nineteenth Century*:

> "from the gifted pen of Dr A. Conan Doyle of Southsea on 'The Geographical Distribution of British Intellect', which. . . will be read with keen interest wherever the English language is spoken".

Whatever had motivated the enthusiastic doctor to embark upon this curious exercise, goodness knows. Some stray remark dropped in conversation, perhaps, or just an idea that occurred to him while looking up some reference work. What he had attempted to do was to analyse the life histories of all the prominent men of the Victorian period (women, naturally, would not come into it), and list them against their counties of birth, to see which county had produced the most. His conclusion was that in the south of England, Hampshire came out top ("scarcely more satisfying or gratifying" wrote the *Hampshire Telegraph*), and Cornwall the lowest, but that over Britain as a whole it was the lowland district of Scotland which was:

> "in the proud position of having reared a larger number of famous men in the later Victorian era than any other stretch of country of similar size".

Perhaps we should not be too surprised at that, coming as it did from an Edinburgh man, though of course he did not include himself in his statistics.

The *Hampshire Telegraph*, as we have noticed, was enthusiastic over this latest example of the literary doctor's versatility. One can almost imagine a little exchange taking place between doctor and editor, on the following lines:

> Editor: "Amazing, Doctor! How did you discover all this?"
> Doctor: "Elementary, my dear Editor. From an inspection of the biographies, and by looking up the Gazetteer".

It was again left to the alert *Hampshire Post* to present a more thoughtful criticism of Dr Doyle's analysis. In a two-column leader headed HAMPSHIRE CELEBRITIES on 10 August it queried many of his conclusions. It invited him to state exactly what criteria he had used for his identification of prominent men; was it excellence in the arts, literature, trade, politics, or merely social status? Why did his list of intellectuals not include any academics? What were the exact dates used to define this period? By using such authorities as the Dictionary of National Biography for his purely empirical research, he had in any case left the onus of selection to these authorities themselves. The paper put forward half a dozen names of its own, and asked why had these not been included. It concluded:

> "Dr Doyle has exhibited great ingenuity and admirable application and patience; and if the result of his labours do not prove perfectly satisfactory, it is only because complete success under the circumstances was out of the question".

Dr Doyle, somewhat chastened perhaps but nevertheless sticking to his guns, replied in a letter the following week. After dealing with a number of points of detail, he ended:

"I am quite ready to admit that results got in this way are to some extent arbitrary, and by no means final. They may, however, serve as a basis for more extended researches by some more competent workman. My inferences are open to criticism; but my facts have not yet been in the smallest degree shaken... It is a curious fact that, among the two hundred leaders which have appeared in the Provincial press upon the subject, every paper agreed that, however badly I treated its own particular county, I have done more than justice to its neighbours. Yours faithfully, A. Conan Doyle, Bush Villa".

Two hundred leaders in the Provincial press? How did he know this? Had he seen them all? Had he actually counted them up? Is this another piece of Doylean one-upmanship? One is reminded of how Sherlock Holmes would casually drop a figure into his conversation to impress the gullible Watson (and his readers). "The fourth smartest man in London", he says of John Clay in *The Red-Headed League*, for instance (Sherlockians like to argue about who were the first three). In *The Reigate Squires* he points out to certain features in the handwriting on a torn scrap of paper which indicate that the words were written alternately by a father and son, then adds:

"I am only, of course, giving you the leading results now of my examination of the paper. There were twenty-three other deductions which would be of more interest to experts than you".

One enthusiast has even worked out what these other twenty-three were. Sherlock Holmes, like his creator, was a man who always liked to come out on top.

With all this going on it may seem a wonder that Dr Doyle found any time at all for cricket. It was in any case a poor summer. July was cold and wet, with very little sunshine and the heaviest rainfall for the month since 1815. August Bank Holiday lived up to the worst of its reputation — pouring rain everywhere, thunderstorm damage in Kent and serious floods in Essex. The membership of the Portsmouth Cricket Club was enhanced by the inclusion of L.G. Bonham-Carter, a free-scoring batsman; Major Bethune, a bowler who could also bat; and a serving Company Sergeant-Major of the Royal Engineers, Jeffkins, who was an all-rounder of much the same class as J.H. Smith, the Grammar School pro. On one or two occasions Dr Doyle unselfishly put himself down as far as seven or eight in the batting order, to give the new members more scope. Even so he managed to achieve a creditable fourth place in the averages, with 17.9 from 26 innings and a highest score of 49. His improving bowling brought him up to second place, with 29 wickets for an average of only 7.3 runs each.

The Club had only one match at the end of May and two in June,

so he kept his hand in by turning out once or twice for Southsea
Rovers. In the Hampshire Cup Portsmouth started well by beating
Havant with an unusually high score, 435 runs to 119 (Jeffkins 135,
Bethune 62, Smith 82, Doyle 10). In a replay of the semi-final on 29
August (the first match having been abandoned, rain stopped play),
they beat Southampton by 145 to 115, but unfortunately had the tables
turned on them in the final. This was a three-day match played away
against Winchester on Friday, Saturday and Monday, 14-17 September,
in refreshingly warm weather. Dr Doyle found time from his surgery
to take part, but in spite of putting out a strong side including Jeffkins,
Bonham-Carter and A.H. Wood Portsmouth were unable to match
Winchester's fourth innings total of 370:

> "It is to be hoped that more support will be given the Club next
> season",

reported the *Portsmouth Times* regretfully.

At Havant a Ladies versus Gentlemen cricket match was played, in
front of a large number of appreciative spectators. The ladies won by
three runs, the gentlemen being restricted to batting with broom
handles, and using only their left hand in bowling and fielding. It must
have been an engaging sight, with the men in their straw boaters
swiping wildly, and the ladies hopping about in their ankle-length
dresses and floppy hats.

Other items too occupied the news that summer. The Reverend S.T.
Briscoe, second master at the Grammar School and another keen
cricketer, preached his farewell sermon as a curate of St Thomas's
before leaving to become Vicar of Linwood, Lincolnshire. Norman
Pares celebrated his promotion to Briscoe's vacancy by getting
married. And Louise discovered she was pregnant. This revelation of
the powers of Nature and the normal cycle of creativity did nothing to
diminish the good doctor's interest in other matters. On 29 September
it was reported that the opening meeting had been held at the Trinity
schoolrooms, Northam Road, Southampton, of the Hampshire
Psychical Society, "the most recent of the scientific societies of the
country". Its objects were stated to be the investigation of various rare
and obscure phenomena, such as hypnotism, thought transference and
allied conditions, and anyone having experience of the same was
invited to write in to the Society giving details. The President was
named as Lieutenant-Colonel G.L. le M. Taylor, of Farnborough, and
one of its three Vice-Presidents was A. Conan Doyle MD of Southsea.
The others were Professor W.F. Barrett FRSE, of the Royal College of
Science, Dublin, and the Honorable Percy Wyndham, of Salisbury.
Where or under what circumstances Dr Doyle first met these gentlemen is not stated; he may not have been attending many more seances
at this time, but his interest in the supernatural was permanent.

On a more local and easily understood matter, an indignant gentleman wrote to the *Portsmouth Times* as follows:

"DEGRADING SCENE AT PORTSEA. Sir, This evening, about 6.30, as I was proceeding to the Harbour station, my attention was drawn to a scene which I have often noticed here before, but never in so aggravated a form... A boy, half naked, covered and bedaubed with slime from head to foot, so much so that his features could not be distinguished, was wallowing in the mud close to the pier and soliciting coppers to be thrown him by the bystanders and passers-by, in order that he might wallow for their delectation in trying to find them... Although I have come across many tribes of savages, and have seen most of the primitive forms of civilisation, I must confess to never having witnessed such a disgusting sight... I trust the publication of this letter may do something to check such degrading scenes.

Faithfully yours,

W.J. Henderson, Captain RN".

Captain Henderson's letter did nothing of the kind, for the Mudlarks were an entertaining, and on the whole harmless (except to their mothers) feature of the Pompey scene right up to the 1960s, until alterations to the Hard — and the increasing affluence of teenagers, maybe — eventually drove them away.

About this time, too, residents in and around Elm Grove began writing to the papers complaining of the activities of unscrupulous builders who were cutting down the trees to make room for more houses. It didn't do them any good, either. Motor traffic and shop development have banished the elms altogether, just as the Dutch disease has killed off all those on the Common.

At Fareham there was an outbreak of military hooliganism. Some soldiers of the Southern Irish Division of the Royal Artillery ran amok and were duly charged with being drunk and disorderly, resisting arrest and assaulting the police. The *Portsmouth Times*, which had got into the habit of inserting headlines into the middle of its sentences, reported thus:

"In one case, having been advised by P.S. King to go home, prisoner retorted that 'he should go home when he liked, and if they wanted anything they could have it', interlarding his remarks with a few adjectives. A number of soldiers came up and UNBUTTONED THEIR BELTS. Prisoner resisted and threw his arms about. He was taken to the station, outside of which soldiers and civilians shouted and hooted.

P.S. KING SPAT BLOOD. Magistrates found the case proved, and sentenced him to one month's hard labour."

September shaded into October, and a disproportionate amount of space in the local papers began to be taken up by reports from London of a series of horrible murders of street women in Whitechapel. There had been four to date. Suspicion was directed against an unknown individual described as "Leather Apron". At the British Association meeting in Bath the scientists diverted themselves with a discussion on the question of the wearing of waist-bands and stays by fashionably dressed ladies. Professor Roy and Mr Adams — treating the subject purely from a physiological view, of course — supported the desirability of wearing some band round the waist, but were not in favour of tight lacing. This opinion was stoutly combatted by several doctors and ladies, who denounced the wearing of stays at all, and described tight lacing as a curse, morally as well as medically. The wearing of stays and tight lacing found an advocate, however, in Miss Lydia Becker, who held that for a woman to be comfortably dressed she must have on well-fitting stays, well laced. The discussion, says the report, caused considerable amusement. What a pity they did not give us a picture of the thoroughly modern Miss Becker, holding forth so boldly on the properties of her underwear. No such intimate matters seem to have engaged the attention of the members of the Portsmouth Literary and Scientific Society. A gentleman did once give a lecture on Vital Statistics, but it turns out that what he was talking about was birth and death rates, not measurements.

Other Societies were still flourishing. The Portsmouth and Gosport Natural History Society, under the more or less permanent direction of General Drayson, met regularly at the Albert Hall in Commerical Road. General Cox and Percy Boulnois were among its members, but not Dr Doyle. Early in October the Southsea Amateur Photographic Society held its first annual meeting in the rooms of Mr G. Farney Brown at 3, Kings Road. Lothian Bonham-Carter was President, and a Dr F. Lord the Honorary Secretary, but again there is no mention of Dr Doyle's name in the newspaper report of the meeting. The rooms were handy enough, just across the street from Bush Villa, and he certainly had not abandoned his interest in photography, for he was busy with his camera in his later years in London and Switzerland. Perhaps he really was feeling the pressure of other matters; perhaps the time of the meeting just coincided with his evening surgery hours. What he did find time for, however, was to read his paper on Carlyle to the Portsmouth Jewish Literary and Debating Society, in their hall at the Queen Street Synagogue. Dr Stern proposed the vote of thanks, and a Mr S. Levy was in the chair.

The Reverend Lindsay Young was in the news again, as he usually contrived to be around the time of Guy Fawkes night and the Orange marches. The latest target of his spleen was the Church of England Working Mens' Society. At a recent local meeting the President of the

Southampton branch of this body had innocently dropped the remark that its members should link together for their mutual well-being and "for the good of the Church Catholic". This was too much for the guardian of non-conformism and anti-Popery, and on 2 November the *Portsmouth Times* printed a letter from him spelling out over nearly a column and a half a dire warning against all the activities of the CEWMS, which he had incontrovertible proof was a Romanising body. A mild defence from three supporters of the Society only served to generate an even longer outburst of vicious prose from the Reverend, attacking Catholicism in general and particularly the practice of confession:

> "The comfort and absolution is by the ministry of the word, not the 'I absolve thee' of a priest, not the filthy cross-examination of a priest who with his array of obscene questions is an incarnation of Satan. . . " etc.

In London, the body of Mary Jane Kelly, eighth victim of the Whitechapel Killer, was found. Sherlock Holmes, however, was very far from Dr Doyle's thoughts at this time for he was preparing his next paper for the Literary Society, to be read on 20 November. His subject was the Portsmouth author George Meredith (not the historian Gibbon, as he states in *Memories and Adventures*). Meredith came from a family of naval tailors but he liked to conceal the fact. His grandfather, bearing the splendid name Melchisedek, must often have made uniforms for some of Nelson's officers in his workshop at 73 High Street, but George, when asked where he came from, preferred to reply "near Petersfield". His books have their humorous side, especially when satirising manners and social conventions, but he cultivated an elaborate turn of phrase which unfortunately could have the effect of obscuring his meaning. Like his remarks on Carlyle, Dr Doyle's praise of Meredith did not meet with universal acceptance among his audience. Dr James Watson was one who got up to say that he personally did not think much of Meredith as a writer, and that in thirty years' time he was sure that he would have fewer readers than he had then. Headmaster Jerrard, in the chair, got the best laugh of the evening by relating a story from his own schooldays. The novelist had visited his school one day, and, as often happens with distinguished visitors, had been asked by a deputation of boys to demand a half-holiday for them. Meredith declined, but said he would write a poem for them instead, which he promptly did. Not being able to understand what he had written, they took the poem to a master, who found that he couldn't make it out either. They decided between them, therefore, to construe the cryptic verse as a disguised request for a half day, and so got what they wanted.

Conan Doyle himself had a similar experience at a later date when he met Meredith in person, as he relates in *Memories and Adventures*:

"I remember that once in the presence of Barrie, Quiller-Couch and myself, he read out a poem which he had inscribed 'To the British Working-Man' in the *Westminster Gazette*. I don't know what the British working-man made of it, but I am sure that we three were greatly puzzled as to what it was about".

In *The Boscombe Valley Mystery* Sherlock Holmes whiles away an evening in the Hereford Arms by lecturing Dr Watson on the subject of George Meredith.

At the next meeting on 4 December both Mrs and Miss Doyle are shown as being present besides the doctor. This was no doubt one of his sisters Connie or Lottie, spending a welcome break from her job as a governess. It was at this meeting, too, that the first intrepid lady member, a Mrs Capel, was elected.

On 18 December Percy Boulnois gave a talk on Some Triumphs of Modern Engineering, instancing such marvels as the Suez and Panama Canals and the Forth Bridge, and ending up with, yes, his own speciality, Sanitary Engineering. In the discussion Dr Doyle raised a laugh when he said he took exception to the Eiffel Tower, which he considered a gigantic act of vandalism, dwarfing as it did all the beautiful public buildings of Paris, and looking like nothing so much as "a huge thing for holding poker and tongs".

He had good reason for taking a cheerful view of things at this time. In September a Portsmouth magazine called *The Crescent* had given him a full-page review, including a rare portrait showing him equipped with a pair of long side-burns (later removed). The article listed the titles of more than a dozen of his published short stories, credited *A Study in Scarlet* with a world-wide reputation, and mentioned his other local and sporting interests. It concluded:

Bush Villa
Southsea

Dear Sir —
I beg to present to the Town Library a copy of my "Mystery of Cloomber" bound in the same way as the "Study in Scarlet" which I sent last year.

Yours faithfully

A. Conan Doyle: M.D.

Jan 16th/89.

Facsimile of Conan Doyle's letter dated 16 January, 1889, presenting a copy of his book *The Mystery of Cloomber* to Portsmouth Library.

"Considering the comparatively short time he has been amongst us, his tall, athletic, broad-shouldered figure is extremely familiar to a large number of Portsmouth people".

Besides this, the publishers Ward and Downey had just brought out *The Mystery Of Cloomber* as a shilling shocker, following the completion of its serialisation in the *Pall Mall* magazines. This did not bring him any more money, but at least gave him the satisfaction of presenting a copy to the Portsmouth Public Library. The book may no longer be there, but a facsimile copy of his letter has been preserved.

Best of all, *Micah Clarke* had been accepted. After four refusals, which nearly caused the author to despair, it had been taken up by Longmans, and was expected to be out fairly early in the coming year. For the first time he had a proper author's contract giving him a royalty of ten per cent on the selling price of six shillings; 7 ½ d, or 3p a time. Not a fortune, but a big step in the right direction. He was on the way to his first literary success. Why, he might even think of getting out *The Firm Of Girdlestone & Co* again.

Chapter VIII

1889 - Holmes and Watson Again

AT THE END of January Louise had her baby. It seems to have been a good time for Literary Society births, for within the space of a fortnight the wives of Dr Claremont, Dr Guillebard and Percy Boulnois all had babies too. While the other husbands inserted the announcement in all the weekly papers, Dr Doyle chose the *Evening News* for his:

> "CONAN DOYLE. On the 28th instant, at Bush Villa, Elm Grove, Mrs Conan Doyle, wife of A. Conan Doyle MD, of a daughter".

The curious formula "of a daughter" was universal practice then. After all, you were announcing the arrival of an individual — what other preposition would you use?

Louise, like the other mothers, had her baby at home. Who then was her medical attendant? John Dickson Carr asserts plainly that it was Dr Doyle himself:

> "Her father, who attended Touie as he had dealt with hundreds of other confinements, confessed himself awestruck and bewildered when the child was his own".

Is this really true? I had always thought that medical etiquette forbad a doctor to attend his own family. Nowadays it has become fashionable for a husband to be present at his wife's confinement. Both my own sons have done so. Luckily it was not the case in my time; the very idea horrifies my wife even now, just as it did Queen Victoria in her time. In 1893 at South Norwood, when Louise was showing the first signs of consumption, Dr Doyle immediately called in both a local GP and a specialist to see her. In one of his medical short stories, *The Curse of Eve*, he portrays most graphically the different mental states of the panic-stricken father and the experienced, matter-of-fact doctor. Surely he could not act both parts himself, or subdue the one effectively by the other. He never mentions in any of his writings who was his own family doctor in Southsea. Dr Claremont perhaps, who was to take over his patients when he left at the end of 1890? Dr Watson? — unlikely, I suggest. My guess is that it would be their friendly neighbour Dr Pike who remained upstairs, while the father was sent down to keep out of the way and calm himself with a smoke and a brandy. Dr Pike had the right qualities of seniority and experience: he had attended the Hawkins family ever since their arrival in Southsea, and had been instrumental in bringing the baby's parents together in the first place. It would be the least they could do, to leave the safety of Louise and her child in his hands.

The baby was named Mary Louise, after her mother and grandmother. Not a lot is known about her. Conan Doyle mentioned the event affectionately but briefly, almost in passing, in his autobiography: "One daughter, Mary had been born to us, our household was a happy one — ", and his other biographers have done likewise. The little girl seems to have been cast much more in the mould of her mother than her masterful father — loving, obedient, subservient to him at all times. In a long life she never married. For much of her early childhood she was more in the company of her grandmother than her mother, when Louise was confined to bed with TB. In later years she did not accompany her father and his family on his world-wide lecture tours, but remained behind faithfully looking after his psychic bookshop in London.

There was a delay of eighteen months before little Mary Louise's birth was properly solemnised; her baptism, certified by her father and the Reverend E.P. Grant, Vicar of Portsmouth, is dated 7 July 1890. There seems no obvious reason for this, even making allowance for her father's religious scruples; after all, he and Louise had been married according to Church of England rites, and it would have been unreasonable to deny the same to their child. The baptismal certificate gives her full surname "Conan Doyle", as was the case with all Dr Doyle's other children. As may have been noticed, in contrast to Americans who like to have a middle initial (even if, as in President Truman's case, it doesn't stand for anything), the Victorian fashion was to put the initial first and have a double surname, as in J. Ward Cousins, H. Percy Boulnois, H. Lindsay Young etc.

We have now arrived at the period when Dr Doyle's literary work, though still to his mind a sideline, was beginning to rival his medical and other activities in keeping his name before the public, if not in consuming his time as well. Already in December and January he was occupying himself in concocting a dramatised version of *A Study in Scarlet*, under the title *Angels of Darkness*. It had some reference to the Mormon episode of the original, but was never completed, let alone published — luckily for Sherlockian students, for it features Dr Watson in some strange adventures in California which would be very difficult to reconcile with his later history.

On 5 January the *Hampshire Telegraph* noticed the book publication of *The Mystery Of Cloomber*:

"This, the latest work from the facile pen of Dr Conan Doyle, of Southsea, which had the good fortune of making its first appearance in the columns of the *Pall Mall Budget*, may be most fittingly described as a fascinating story. Nothing delights the novel-reader of the present day more than mystery, and when, as in the book under review, it is hedged round by the forces of the supernatural, he is more than satisfied... It is far removed from the well-worn track affected by novelists, the plot is striking and original, the incidents new and strange, and the climax weirdly tragical... In our opinion the construction of this story is an improvement upon that of *A Study in Scarlet*, which although deservedly popular, lacks dramatic sequence, and it will add materially to the growing reputation of Dr Doyle".

The author may have been pleased to see this, but not many people would agree with the reviewer's last sentence now.

Then on 25 February the first copies of *Micah Clarke* appeared in the shops. The *Evening News* was quick to notice, and published a long and enthusiatic review by Hugh MacLaughlan on 4 March:

"Dr Conan Coyle has gone at one stride into the front rank of novelists. His latest book *Micah Clarke* is not only *his* best; it is the best historical novel that has been published for years. The *Study in Scarlet* was good — Sherlock Holmes being a real addition to the men we know — but both this and its successor *The Mystery of Cloomber* compared with *Micah Clarke* were studies in fiction, the necessary preparation for a great effort. Dr Conan Doyle has now passed through the initial stage, and has made his first important step in the right direction and at the right time... lighting up one of the most romantic periods of our national life with his own inimitable character painting and fascinating powers in the description of places and events. We do not say this because Dr Conan Doyle is a resident of Portsmouth. A man's town is generally the last place to recognise his capacity..."

This review was repeated, with additions, in the *Hampshire Telegraph* of 9 March, which concluded:

"Dr Conan Doyle must have taken infinite pains to be accurate in his types... The reputation of Dr Conan Doyle as a writer of fiction will be immensely enhanced by *Micah Clarke*".

The *Portsmouth Times* also took notice on the same day, but contented itself by reprinting the review from *The Globe* newspaper, slightly more critical in tone:

"In *Micah Clarke* (Longmans & Co) by Dr A. Conan Doyle, we meet with an historical story of the kind delightful to imaginative lads, and acceptable to those of their elders who have retained some youthful feeling. . . There is no 'plot' in the work, and there is next to no female interest — facts which, while they will deter many, will attract others, and certainly make *Micah Clarke* all the better reading for the young. . . The frivolous and the ignorant will not care for *Micah Clarke*, but the thoughtful and fairly well read will recognise at once the care and ability of the author".

On 6 April the *Portsmouth Times* returned to the subject with an interesting review from *The World*:

"Dr Conan Doyle has taken the same period of English history for his *Micah Clarke* as Mr Besant has taken in his *For Faith and Freedom*. . . and if a comparison there must be, we frankly own to preferring Dr Doyle's. Indeed, his story strikes us as quite the best thing of its kind that has been done since *Lorna Doone*, a most brisk and entertaining chapter of romance. . . The scene on Sedgemoor, and especially the charge of the Royal cavalry out of the mist upon the rebel flank, is a right good battle-piece".

Micah Clarke did well. Already on 16 April the *Evening News* announced to its readers that:

"those who have read Dr Conan Doyle's last novel, *Micah Clarke*, will be more pleased than surprised to learn that the first edition is sold out, and that the publishers, Messrs Longmans, are about to issue another."

By the end of the following year it had sold 6000 copies, leaving its author nearly £200 to the good, and the first school edition came out in 1894.

In between his other activities and the cares of his new family, Dr Doyle still found time for his winter recreation on the football field. The Portsmouth Club had fixtures on most Saturdays in January and February. They now had three men of the name Seddon playing regularly; F.J. at centre half (Captain, and a County player), and brothers E. and G. forming the left half of the forward line. A.H. Wood often played too, except in Cup matches. Unfortunately they were knocked out of the Portsmouth Challenge Cup in one of the early rounds. It was the Grammar School side which actually reached the Final in this competition; they lost to Geneva Cross, a Southampton team, by the only goal and so the Cup, for the first time, left its home town. Portsmouth, on the other hand, now got as far as the Final of the Hampshire Cup, having beaten the Grammar School 2-0 in the semi-final. The match, against a Royal Engineers team from Aldershot, was played in front of a crowd of several thousand spectators at Southampton on 2 March, a cold, frosty day. The *Evening News* reported A.C. Smith in his usual position at back, but the *Hampshire Telegraph* identified him as Dr A.C. Doyle. The soldiers were too strong, however, and took the Cup back to Aldershot after winning 5-1.

There were Liberal-Unionist Committee meetings for Dr Doyle to attend — A.J. Balfour, the Chief Secretary for Ireland, was to visit Portsmouth in the summer, and much detailed staff work was needed to be done in preparation — and also his secretarial duties with the Literary Society. He did not attend Mr Weston's talk on Water Purification on 29 January, the evening following the birth of Mary Louise, but was back to hear Staff-Commander Miller on The Straits of Magellan a fortnight later. Very different was the talk given on 26 February, by their guest speaker, the Very Reverend Dr Kitchin, Dean of Winchester. Under the prosaic title "Some Notes on Mediaeval Commerce" the Dean had presented a learned but good-humoured and entertaining narrative of everyday life in England under the reign of Edward III, whom he described as the father of English commerce, from his initiative in introducing Flemish artificers to teach his townspeople the arts of manufacture. He spoke of the rough foods people ate, and the way the crude cereals ground down their teeth, as could be seen from old skulls. The English were great meat-eaters, then as now; a Venetian visitor had reported that so much meat made the people sleepy, but a kind Providence had overrun the country with fleas, and this prevented the people from dying of apoplexy! He described the development of the Craft Guilds, which from their jealously guarded trade secrets and strict demarcation lines he saw as the precursors of modern Trades Unions; and told of the great St Giles fair at Winchester, when for sixteen days the Bishop dismissed the Mayor and constables and ran the city himself from his own market stall. Transport was the greatest difficulty, due to the lack of roads, the crudity of their vehicles, and the prevalence of robbers — Hampshire, said the Dean, was of all counties the most overrun by thieves and cutthroats. When Henry III visited Winchester, two casks of his wine were stolen on the way. The first set of jurors sent out to apprehend the thieves failed to do so, for they knew that they came from among themselves. They were immediately hanged. A second set did not make the same error; over fifty courtiers and other members of the King's retinue were executed.

Dr Doyle listened with great attention. Enthusiastically seconding the vote of thanks, he asked why was not this kind of fascinating detail included in school history books instead of just boring lists of battles and dates. With the success of *Micah Clarke* fresh in his mind, he was already thinking about its successor. *Ivanhoe* had always been his favourite novel of Scott's. Knights in armour, the clash of steel and the glories of physical combat in the cause of chivalry — these were what he wanted to write about now. If he had not already settled on the fourteenth century as the period for his next historical work, this talk of Dr Kitchin's must surely have made up his mind for him.

On a couple of evenings in February the citizens of Southsea were diverted by a demonstration of The New Hypnotism at the Portland Hall arranged by "Professor" Milo de Meyer, a Frenchman. Despite having a limited command of English he put on a show in the best music-hall traditions, getting groups of men from the audience on to the platform to perform ludicrous antics such as putting out an imaginary fire and trying to act as ballet dancers. It was a great success, provocative of no little mirth, as the *Evening News* put it, but the Professor took a serious view of his technique, and the evening before had invited a number of local professional men and journalists to a private demonstration (he called it a seance) to see him describe his method of "Animal Magnetism" more fully — and we don't need to be told which well-known Southsea practitioner had arranged for himself to be included. When they arrived at the Hall they found ten young men already there, waiting. Through his interpreter (one subject M. de Meyer was not a professor of was languages) the professor explained that these had been pre-selected to act as subjects for his experiments, in order to save time. At once a large man got up from the audience and said that he wished to volunteer to be a subject. The Professor looked at the interrupter, who seemed to be about two feet taller than himself, and quickly decided that this was an offer he couldn't refuse. He explained that his method did not rely upon putting the subject to sleep. Instead, he took hold of one of the young men by his hands and drew him forward so that his weight was transferred to the front leg, at the same time gazing into his eyes. When he let go the subject fell on to his knees and remained there, completely unable to rise even with the help of his friends; although still fully conscious he had lost all feeling in his lower limbs, and was stuck fast to the floor until the Professor released him by the odd device of blowing in his face.

> "An attempt to magnetise Dr Doyle in a similar manner failed, the Professor remarking, after making the attempt, that the process would take too long"

reported the *News* (we can imagine the doctor's quiet satisfaction). General Drayson, who now seems to have added amateur mesmerism to the list of his other accomplishments, managed to revive another of the Professor's subjects by blowing at him. Most of M de Meyer's other experiments were highly successful, some of them quite dramatic. One man had a pin thrust through his arm without feeling any pain. One was made to go through the motions of murdering his father in a realistic manner. The Professor even put six of his subjects, purposely engaged in animated conversation, to sleep while he himself was out of the room.

Dr Doyle was fascinated. Murder by remote control — what a capital idea for a story! Not yet, perhaps. Learn a bit more about it first; one shouldn't theorise too much in advance of the facts. The seed would germinate in its time.

On 28 March a show of a different kind was presented when a large number of local ladies and gentlemen put on fancy dress and enacted a series of Tableaux Vivants, in aid of funds for the Eye and Ear Infirmary. Young Master William James got a generous round of applause when he appeared in the blue costume he had worn as the model for "Bubbles", the popular painting by Sir John Millais, his grandfather. Rather more than fifty years later Admiral Sir William James was back in Portsmouth as Naval Commander-in-Chief during some of the worst years of the war. The performance realised a much needed £66 for the Infirmary, and was judged so successful that it was repeated a few weeks later.

This second performance followed immediately after the Annual Meeting of the subscribers to the Infirmary which was held in the Guildhall on 26 March. Richard Ford, other members of his family, the Reverend Desmond, a naval surgeon, and many other supporters were there besides the doctors themselves — though Dr Cousins unfortunately could not be present owing to the death that week of his aged mother at her home in Victoria Road South. The Mayor, Mr George Ellis, regretted that in the year just ended the 140,000 people of Portsmouth could only raise £140 between them; one sovereign per thousand persons. Mr Ford announced that the Infirmary was treating on average one hundred patients a day, and that no fewer than eighty different eye diseases had been encountered. Dr Conan Doyle in his turn bore testimony to the good work so unostentatiously performed in their little Infirmary:

> "To the working man and the mechanic, his eyes were practically his life, and the loss of his eyes a living death".

Then, perhaps overcome by thoughts of the success of *Micah Clarke*, he concluded by asking publicly that he himself might be entered as a subscriber ("Hear, hear!").

That same week Mr Quintrell, Master of the Portsea Island Union Workhouse, received a letter in the following terms:

> "WANTED, A WIFE. Sir, I have taken the liberty of askein you if you can obelige me with a respectele woman that would make a Poor man a good wife. I am a seaman and lost my wife. I got one little girl with me 8 years old, the rest is away to work. I am away in the summer yachting and if you culd sute me with a woman from 35 to 40, sober and not Bad looking, and wants a good husbain i should bee glad to see hur. I am at home from 4 in the evening all

this week, so sirs if you culd low her out to see me at ... st Buckland I shuld be much obelige to you sir. I dont mind ware beain mareid or nor if no children. If you can obelige me I shuld be stremely obelige to you sir so I will close ths note. I remain a friend. I am 46".

In those days, of course, men worked long hours, and domestic work, being carried out by hand was itself so laborious and time-consuming, that a man could not possibly do both for himself. It was a mutual need, as well as mutual affection, which kept a husband and wife together. Disappointingly, one feels, the Board of Guardians did nothing about this homely appeal. They probably had a good laugh, and the letter was left "to lie on the table".

On 18 April, the day before Good Friday, Messrs Penny and Clark got a price of £365 for the sale of No 104 King Street at their King's Road auction rooms. In the same week Mr C.G. Inkpen, of 112 High Street, displayed his new walking-stick camera stand, contrived out of an ordinary walking-stick fitted with a light metal tripod which could be folded into a length of no more than twelve inches.

At the end of the month four married men took themselves off for a week's bachelor holiday in the New Forest. Conan Doyle and Percy Boulnois each had a young baby at home. Vernon Ford, the third member, was five years older than Conan Doyle but had already been married for ten years and five of his six children had been born. Perhaps they all just wanted to get away from their families for a short spell; perhaps, who knows, it was Dr Ford who put up the idea in the first place. With them, as a representative of the senior generation (and maybe even to settle any misgivings that one or other of their wives might have entertained) they took the old campaigner and astronomical expert, General Drayson. Besides, the General was good at cards — had he not written a book about whist? — and that was how they would be spending their evenings. Perhaps, too, one of them was trying out Mr Inkpen's walking-stick camera stand.

They found rooms in the little village of Emery Down, near Lyndhurst. The weather was still cool with a touch of frost at night, as it often is around the turn of May, but the trees were nearly in leaf and the dawn chorus of the birds every morning would remind them that Nature was blooming. Their base was well chosen; central, with grassy paths or gravel lanes radiating outwards to put any part of the Forest within the range of a strong walker. Two miles to the north was the village of Minstead, with its quaintly named inn The Trusty Servant and the little old church where Conan Doyle and his wife now lie buried. Less than a mile further on lay Castle Malwood, an old mansion (now an Electricity Board headquarters) and, across the high road, the stone marking the spot where William Rufus was killed on 2 August 1100, and the inn commemorating the name of the man who shot the fatal arrow, Sir Walter Tyrrell. Nine miles to the south-east was the ruined Abbey of Beaulieu, and two miles beyond that Bucklers Hard, the single row of boat-builders' cottages leading down to the Beaulieu river. A four-mile stroll due south would bring them to the village of Brockenhurst. As far again and they would reach the sea at Lymington, or more to the west in the direction of Christchurch, the village of Hordle, from which one of Conan Doyle's characters was to take his name. Burley was six miles to the west, Ringwood and Fordingbridge eight each. All of them good long walks, over hills, heath and woodland, but well provided at their termini with houses where the explorers could refresh themselves before the return journey. If General Drayson, at the age of sixty-two, could keep up with his companions throughout he would have every reason to feel satisfied with himself (at least he would be too tired to keep them up all night talking about the obliquity of the ecliptic).

All through the week Dr Doyle let his imagination roam freely, soaking in atmosphere, formulating incidents and characters, storing them away in his mind ready for his next burst of creativity. Stimulated as he had been by the Dean of Winchester's lecture, he now had his plot identified; knights, archers, peasants and maidens would be the players, and the New Forest would be their opening scene.

Back home everything was being geared up for the big political event of the year, the visit on 5 June of A.J. Balfour, a future Prime Minister and the man currently charged by the Conservatives with keeping Ireland within the Empire and frustrating any of Mr Gladstone's attempts to give Dublin Home Rule. All the manifold arrangements worked well on the day, and proper credit for their success was given in the papers to the Chairman of the organising committee, R.W. Ford, and his two Honorary Secretaries, Mr J.J. Rockett and Dr A. Conan Doyle. The *Portsmouth Times* published a two-page supplement containing a full account of the proceedings with lengthy reports of all the speeches. The Minister came down by the 11.35 from Waterloo, and was met at the high level platform punctually at 2.08 pm, the steam train of the time taking no longer over the 80-mile journey than today's electric ones. There was an enormous crush of people, but:

> "it was here that the Law and Order branch of the Unionist organisation appeared to the utmost advantage, for in spite of the density of the crowd they preserved a clear course for the honourable gentleman which enabled him to be conveyed without harm to a carriage waiting in the station yard"

and we know whose burly figure would be in charge of that efficient corps of strong-arm stewards. Dr Doyle was with the party the whole day, at the official lunch in the George Hotel, the afternoon visit to the

Conservative Club in Commercial Road, and the great mass meeting in the Amphitheatre at 8 pm; this no doubt, was the occasion when he got his hat squashed. The Minister made an impassioned speech in defence of the current Irish policy, and was wildly applauded after the fashion of political meetings in general. Richard Ford proposed a resolution expressing thanks to the Minister and confidence in his policy, and then it was Dr Doyle's turn. Seconding the resolution, in his best public-address manner, he declared that:

> "they were assembled there that evening on no narrow party basis, but as Englishmen and patriots. . ."

As Englishmen, we note, not Scots or Welsh or even British. Dr James Watson, very much a home-bred Scotsman, when describing his experiences in China in the *Edinburgh Medical Journal*, still entitled his article "The English doctor in southern Manchooria".

> "No soldier who had laid down his life in England's service had played a more patriotic part than the Chief Secretary for Ireland"

went on Dr Doyle amid loud cheers, and more in the same vein. It is fashionable to be a touch cynical about such sentiments nowadays, but we can be sure he meant every word of it at the time.

Dr Doyle's work for the cause may have been briefly interrupted by an item affecting one of his other interests. On Tuesday, 7 May, a Mr John Beaumont of Bournemouth, "a mild and benevolent-looking gentleman, spectacled and possessed of snowy locks and beard", had addressed an audience of 150 persons in the Yorke Rooms, St Paul's Road (just off Elm Grove) on the subject of Spiritualism. His lecture, according to the *Evening News*, constituted:

> "a vigorous denouncement of modern spiritualism as AN OLD SNAKE OF SATAN'S in a new dress".

Unfortunately, he had either planned his speech badly or got carried away by the exuberance of his own verbosity, since:

> "after speaking for an hour and a half, by which time Deuteronomy had been reached in the citation of passages bearing on his subject, Mr Beaumont abruptly broke off, and a second lecture was arranged for Tuesday next".

No names were listed of those who attended the lecture, but it produced a sharp reaction in the shape of a long letter in the *Evening News* of 9 May. Headed "Spiritualism. A Fraud or a Revelation?", it began:

> "Sir, When any new form of knowledge arises above the mental horizon of the human race there are always a certain number of

well-meaning but narrow-minded men who are ready to denounce it as being opposed to Scriptural teaching. Galileo was denounced... Sir Joseph Simpson invented chloroform, and this led to an outcry on the part of many weak-minded but religious people who considered that its use was an interference with the Divine ordinance, that man should be born to pain and sorrow...

"Since all the lines of thought have had to encounter this opposition, it is no wonder that Spiritualism should be no exception. It stands in the curious position, however, of being attacked by two different bodies of men upon diametrically opposite grounds. The agnostic modern-science party refuse absolutely to admit the possibility of spirit communion, and dispute the genuineness of the alleged phenomena. The intolerant religious party, of which Mr Beaumont may stand as a type, admit the possibility, but dispute the morality of the proceeding. Obviously one or other party of our opponents must be wrong. The effect of this double opposition has been that in forty years Spiritualism has spread from an obscure American village over the whole civilised world; that a recent computation has put the number of professed Spiritualists at 30,000,000..."

The writer goes on to deal with the religious objections first, quoting the names of various clergymen who support Spiritualism, and then the Bible:

"From cover to cover the Bible is full of Spiritualism. 'Test the spirits, whether they be of God', says Paul. What is meant by the 'Communion of Saints' save spirit communication with the holy dead?... Is it reasonable to suppose that the all-powerful Creator had given man powers, and implanted in him possiblilites of knowledge, which he is never under any circumstances to use? Had the omnipotent Deity designed that death should be an absolute barrier between this world and the next, would He not have made it so?..."

He then adds his own testament:

"When I speak of Spiritualism I do not mean the public performance of self-styled mediums, which, whether real or simulated, are a pandering to a morbid public curiosity, but I refer to the private seance, where there is no paid medium, no interest in deception, and an atmosphere of solemnity and reverence. Spiritualism is no more to be judged by venal public mediums, than Christianity is to be condemned because in every Church there are a certain number of hypocrites and time-servers".

To counter the scientific agnostics, the writer then lists the names of a dozen "men of scientific attainments who have spent years in investigation under the most rigid test conditions", including Sir William Crookes, Alfred Russel Wallace, Professor Challis the Cambridge astronomer, J.G. Wood the natural history writer, and others. The letter concludes:

> "Death. . . is but a frail partition through which loving hands may meet. A Spiritualist cannot fear death. He knows that it only marks a fresh stage in his ascending course, and opens up for him a wider field of knowledge and of usefulness. . . As to the future, it is in the opinion of many the strongest and most vital movement on this planet. It is not the foe, but the strongest ally of a broad and enlightened Christianity".

The letter was signed, with no address, "Spiritualist". Eight full paragraphs, nearly a column long, with no sign of editorial abridgement. The writer could, I suppose, have been General Drayson, but its trenchant style, the logical presentation of the argument, the quoting of impressive figures, the display of Biblical knowledge, the list of scientific names whom he was known to revere, and the forthright personal statement suggest far more strongly that if not by Arthur Conan Doyle it is an extraordinarily good imitation of him. It is not like Dr Doyle to have used a pseudonym — his interest in psychic matters was, after all, common knowledge — but the strong impression remains that he himself was the author. If this is so, it suggests again that his commitment to the belief was already strong and permanent in his Southsea days.

The following Tuesday, as promised, Mr Beaumont returned to the charge. True Spiritualism was of Christianity, and it was a misnomer as applied to:

> "THIS WORK OF THE DEMONS. Take it all in. You have come to hear and I to speak",

he shouted — unnecessarily, we might think. He invited any Spiritualists in his audience to declare themselves, but got a nil response. At the end, reported the *Evening News*:

> "men, women and children tucked their Bibles under their arms and, with the lecturer, consigned Spiritualism to the father of lies".

There were no further letters, the next topic to engage the attention of the *News's* correspondents being the recent legislation on the muzzling of dogs.

Cricket. It was not the Portsmouth Club's best season. They lost away to Southampton in the first round of the Hampshire Cup, and had very few matches at all in August and September. It was Southsea Rovers who declared themselves the most successful local civilian club at their annual dinner in November. Their Secretary was G. Farney Brown, of the Photographic Society. Dr Doyle managed to play in some of the early games. He got a duck against the United Services, when Portsmouth were crushed by 205 runs to 95, and scored only 6 when opening against the South Lancashire Regiment, just after his return from Emery Down. Top scorer for the side was A.E. Cogswell, who hit 22 after going in at No. 10, but the team still lost. Dr Doyle did better with a score of 26 when playing for Southsea Rovers against the Royal Marine Artillery, but all else paled into insignificance behind his performance against the Royal Artillery on 11 May. Portsmouth won with a total of 228 for 3 wickets, thanks principally to:

> "the magnificent defence of Dr Conan Doyle, the Captain, who made no fewer than 111 not out".

A century! What a splendid prelude to his thirtieth birthday on 22 May.

Perhaps the absence of the Captain had something to do with Portsmouth's lack of fixtures in the late summer, for this was the period when he is said to have gone back alone to the New Forest, there to shut himself up for two or three weeks with a load of history books and to concentrate on his researches for his new novel, to be called *The White Company*. He had the elements of the tale all ready in his head, but if he was to be taken seriously as a historian he felt it was essential to show that he had all the details correct — just as the Dean of Winchester had done in his lecture: the names of the parts, the kind of things people said to one another, the proper way to describe the heraldic devices on their shields, what they called their weapons and the various items of their clothing. In an interview he claimed to have consulted over one hundred and fifty books in his preparation for *The White Company*. As before, we may ask ourselves whether he did actually count them up, but his notebooks leave no doubt as to how seriously he did take his studies.

It was in that month of August that his literary career took another giant leap forward, though in an altogether different direction. The story has been told many times but is worth repeating. The American house of Lippincott's, based in Philadelphia, had sent one of their men, J.M. Stoddart, over to England to search out some new talent. Lippincott's published a monthly magazine in both countries, and their policy was to include a complete story in each number. Stoddart called upon James Payn, editor of *The Cornhill*, and Payn recommended him to try Dr Conan Doyle of Southsea. The result was the celebrated dinner for four at the Langham Hotel, Portland Place with Stoddart, Doyle, Oscar Wilde, and an Irish MP called Gill. Nobody seems very sure as to what the MP's part in the meeting was — perhaps he was just brought in by Stoddart as a fellow Irishman and an entertaining conversationalist. Dr Doyle has left on record his impressions of Wilde:

"His conversation left an indelible impression upon my mind. He towered above us all, and yet had the art of seeming to be interested in all that we could say. He had delicacy of feeling and tact, for the monologue man, however clever, can never be a gentleman at heart. He took as well as gave, but what he gave was unique. He had a curious precision of statement, a delicate flavour of humour, and a trick of small gestures to illustrate his meaning, which was peculiar to himself... I should add that never in Wilde's conversation did I observe one trace of coarseness of thought, nor could one at that time associate him with such an idea... I thought at the time, and still think, that the monstrous development which ruined him was pathological, and that a hospital rather than a police court was the place for its consideration".

The upshot of the meeting was that Wilde set to work on *The Picture of Dorian Gray*, and Dr Doyle agreed to write a new Sherlock Holmes story. On the train back to Portsmouth, his spirits must have been high. For the first time in his writing career a publisher had actually approached him and requested a work. Was this to be the end of hawking his wares around the country, the anxious days and weeks of waiting for yet another polite rejection? The arrangement was that he was to receive £100 in return for not less than 40,000 words, the manuscript to be delivered not later than January, and that was just for the magazine copy. There could be book publication and serial rights to follow. Ideas for the new tale were already crowding into his head: the stolen treasure, the body in a locked attic room, an assassin with abnormal powers — not an ape, that would be too obvious a copy from Poe's *Murders in The Rue Morgue*, but, yes, an acrobatic native, a pigmy (his small footprints would give him away) — and so the game would be afoot once more. Back home he set to work at once, pushing thoughts of the Middle Ages out of the way for the time being. In barely a month he had completed the manuscript and *The Sign of Four* was on its way to Lippincott by early October. This is the one which ends up with Dr Watson getting married, and Holmes stretching out his long, white hand for the cocaine-bottle. It was written so quickly that the author didn't even have time to organise his dates properly; the action starts in early July, yet later the same day we are told it is a September evening — to the everlasting confusion of Sherlockian experts, who like to establish the exact dates of all the adventures. Dr Watson, too, is given a wounded leg, although we are told in *A Study in Scarlet* that it was his shoulder which was damaged in Afghanistan. The urchins of the Baker Street Irregulars appear again. There is a character patterned after Oscar Wilde, and the Langham Hotel gets a mention (as it does in two other Holmes adventures). The climax of the story is an exciting chase down the river Thames in a police launch, only to find that the villains have jettisoned the treasure into the mud off the Plumstead Marshes. It is a trip which the enthusiasts of the London Sherlock Holmes Society have already made twice, still without finding any of the treasure. It seems unlikely that they will ever get it back now.

Holmes has now added drug-taking to his other eccentricities; a seven per cent solution of cocaine, injected into his arm three times a day. It may be no coincidence here that the British Dental Association had held its annual conference in Portsmouth the previous year. There had been much discussion on the uses and effects of cocaine. Dr R.E. Power, Medical Officer at Portsmouth Convict Prison, related a story of how he had carried out a leg amputation under cocaine, and the patient appeared to enjoy the sensation so much that at its termination he said he wished he could have another limb treated under similar conditions. Dr Doyle, no stranger to self-experimentation himself, would have been sure to take notice.

Holmes reports that his practice has extended recently to the Continent, and we are introduced to his famous monograph enumerating the difference between the ashes of one hundred and forty forms of cigar, cigarette and pipe tobaccos (did he smoke them all himself?). The opening includes one of the classic examples of his deductive processes in which, merely from an examination of a pocket watch, he infers the history of Watson's elder brother:

"He was a man of untidy habits — very untidy and careless. He was left with good prospects, but he threw away his chances, lived for some time in poverty with occasional short intervals of prosperity, and , finally, taking to drink, he died. That is all I can gather".

Here is the essence of Conan Doyle's inventiveness; and if nowadays we think this kind of thing is corny, the answer is simple: just try inventing a few more.

Dr Watson is allowed to fall in love and become engaged to Mary Morstan, the heroine, in a very offhand sort of way. Hardly more than a couple of paragraphs are alloted to chart the course of their romance — which Dr Doyle perhaps thought it wise to include in response to previous complaints by publishers that his stories had no interest for female readers. It provides the opportunity for Holmes to make one of his most characteristic pronouncements:

"Love is an emotional thing, and whatever is emotional is opposed to that true, cold reason which I place above all things. I should never marry myself, lest I bias my judgement".

It is also interesting to note from Watson's remark:

"I fear that it may be the last investigation in which I shall have the chance of studying your methods"

— that even now, at the end of the second Sherlock Holmes story, Conan Doyle still had no thought that there would be any more to follow.

In Portsmouth itself the citizens on their daily to-ings and fro-ings across the town centre were able to witness the gradual uprising of their splendid new Guildhall. Like many another building contract before and since, the work had got behind time; the building should have been completed by October, three years from the date of laying the foundation stone, but it would now be well into 1890 before it was ready. Still, there was already enough on view to show the true scale of this new symbol of municipal pride — by Bolton out of Leeds Town Hall, but wider, longer, higher and more ornamented than either. The clock tower was up, and the skeleton framework of three great flights of steps could be seen.

Transport was in the news. A new schedule of ferry services from Southsea to Cowes was announced. Mr A.W. White revealed that in addition to his many other interests he was Secretary of the Clarence Pier Esplanade Company. The Southsea Railway was still not making a profit for its shareholders, but a direct line to Southampton via Netley was opened at the beginning of September. Clever people wrote to the press, as they do now, pointing out anomalies in the fare structures. "Regular Traveller" informed readers of the *Portsmouth Times* that by buying an ordinary return from Portsmouth to Fareham (1s-4d) and then one from Fareham to Winchester (2s-8d) you could save sixpence on the through fare from Portsmouth to Winchester of 4s-6d return. In London the dockers were on strike, but at Southampton they were working round the clock to cope with the volume of traffic from the P & O, Royal Mail, and Union steamship lines. The day rate of pay was fivepence an hour, the night rate sixpence, but the London men had been out for weeks trying to get sixpence as the day rate.

A new enterprise was revealed on 12 October with the publication of a prospectus for a Portsmouth and South Hampshire Electricity Supply Company. Readers were invited to subscribe towards the capital of £37,500, in 7,500 Ordinary shares of £5 each, for the purpose of building a central generating station for the supply of electricity to the town and its environs. The list of Directors included many well-known local names: John Pares JP, Julian Bonham-Carter JP, E. Galt, R.W. Ford, W.H. Handley, A.W. White. R.W. Ford and Son were the Solicitors to the Company; D.M. Ford was Company Secretary. A list of Founder Subscribers was published; besides the above it contained the names not only of Axford and Knott, two of the more affluent doctors, but also that of A. Conan Doyle Esq. MD of Bush Villa, who had applied for 50 ordinary shares and one Founder's share, total cost £255. If his practice was still only bringing in £300 a year, this now suggests that

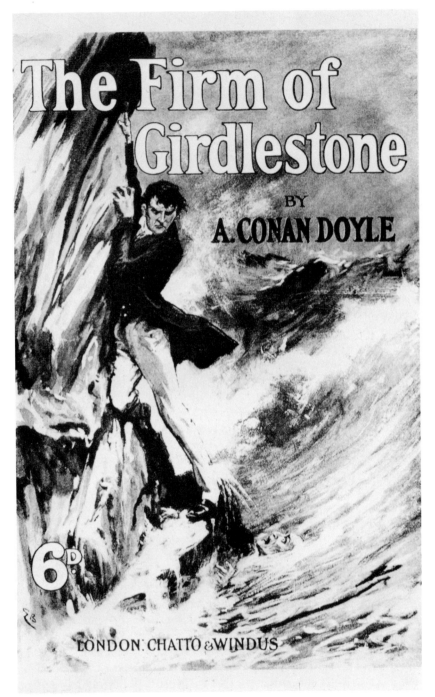

The Firm of Girdlestone Conan Doyle's first full-length adventure story, written during his time at Southsea.

literature was beginning to rival medicine as a source of income. Not only was he in funds from *Micah Clarke* and *The Sign of Four.* Encouraged by the success of these two, he had unearthed *The Firm Of Girdlestone & Co* from its drawer and got it accepted by the Globe Newspaper Syndicate. It was serialised in the London newpaper *The People,* and then published in book form by Chatto and Windus the following year. It remains an unjustly neglected work today, far better than *The Mystery Of Cloomber.* His investment in the new Electricity Company unfortunately did not turn out to be very profitable, for the Corporation took over the whole project in 1892.

Once again religious controversy invaded the correspondence columns of the *Evening News.* On 10 November the Reverend Reginald N. Shutte, Vicar of St Michael's, had preached a long and impassioned sermon on a text taken from Chapter 36 of the Old Testament prophet Jeremiah, beginning:

> "This word came to Jeremiah from the Lord, saying, Take thee a roll of a book, and write therein all the words that I have spoken unto thee. . . "

The Reverend Shutte was a popular and worthy pastor who had done much practical work in his parish, including for example setting up a mission for fallen women in the worst brothel area of Portsea, but he was also a Ritualist of the old school, a stickler for ceremonial and procedure — he even insisted on segregating the sexes in his congregations. The message of his sermon was that the Bible was literally the Word of God. The Bible was perfect, without contradiction or flaw, and unless we received it as such we were utterly lost, and for ever. He seems to have had as good a flow of words as the Reverend Lindsay Young, though differently directed, and vigorously denounced all criticism or questioning of the Bible, however slight or well meant, as "the trash and filth of atheistic teachers".

The first reaction appeared on Monday 18 November in the shape of a long letter from "Broad Churchman", who not surprisingly took exception to Mr Shutte's over-literal interpretation of the Word:

> "A day is coming, yea, even now is come, when men are beginning to see things differently, and in the new reformation which is coming one of the most remarkable changes we shall see will be the new use that men make of the Bible. . ."

The following day three letters, signed respectively "A Southsea Curate", "Katholikor", and Thomas Gain, all criticised "Broad Churchman" in his turn for being too literal in his interpretation of the Reverend Shutte's words, and for doubting the Bible's inspiration by God. Then on the Wednesday a fifth correspondent joined in, with a letter which began:

"Sir, — I have read with much interest the very moderate letter of
'Broad Churchman' and the answers which it has called forth. From
my own point of view he errs rather in the direction of narrowness
than of breadth, but it is well that every phrase of religious thought
should have its champions. From the friction of many views a spark
of truth may be elicited — "

The writer went on to reprimand "A Southsea Curate" for
upholding the idea of absolute inspiration of the Bible when it
contained statements which we knew to be wrong:

"Was it the Deity who was the author of the statement that the
world was created in six days, that the creation was some five
thousand years ago?. . . If it was, then alas for our conceptions of the
Deity —"

His letter then concluded:

"Winwood Reade in his 'Martyrdom of Man' remarks that at the
time of the Reformation men pulled down idols of stone and wax,
in order to put up in their place an idol of paper and printer's ink.
Let us take the good of the Bible and make the most of it, but let
us, in the name of reverence and reason, forbear from ascribing to
the All-wise that which would represent him as a magnified man,
full of the petty angers, jealousies and revenges which we condemn
in our fellow mortals. We need no book and no inspiration to tell
us of His wisdom and His power. The starry heavens, where a
hundred million worlds are circling above us, are enough to bring
it home to us far more closely than the words of any Jewish prophet,
and there is a moral sense within us which guides the agnostic as
well as the Christian. The broader our views the better. . .
Yours faithfully, A Southsea Physician".

If the style and the sentiments of that letter are not enough in
themselves to provide a positive identification of "A Southsea
Physician", two further points should remove any lingering doubts.
One is his postscript, with its typical touch of ironic humour:

"P.S. One gentleman, I observe, wants to know how modern thought
is superior to that of the sixteenth century. One sign of progress is
that a discussion of this sort may be courteously carried on without
any of the disputants having the power, or, I hope, the desire, to
make a bonfire of their opponents".

The other lies in a remark made by Sherlock Holmes to Dr Watson
in *The Sign of Four*:

"Let me recommend this book — one of the most remarkable ever
penned. It is Winwood Reade's *Martyrdom of Man*."

The Literary Society opened its new season under the Presidency of Percy Boulnois. There was a very full attendance to hear him give a long history of the development of industrial power, with particular reference to the growth of steam as a source of motive energy, but leading up also to recent advances in the employment of the new medium, electricity, in such devices as the electric telegraph and the phonograph. Dr Conan Doyle, who was there with his wife, wisely chose not to comment. It was the *Hampshire Post*, so knowledgeable in literary matters, which in an editorial gave it as its considered opinion that electricity would never replace steam in the industrial world.

Chapter IX

1890 - Could Go Far

A LOT HAD happened for Dr Doyle in 1889. *Micah Clarke* was in print and well received; *The Sign Of Four* had been dispatched ready for publication; *The Firm Of Girdlestone* too was in print in serial form with book publication to follow. By now he was deep into *The White Company*, writing hard in every spare moment. And if his general practice did not seem to be much larger than it had ever been, he was growing in his experience of treating eye complaints. He must have felt, at the age of thirty, that life was still full of promise; that progress on all fronts was only waiting for him to grasp it. In *Memories and Adventures* he wrote, with reference to his sudden trip to Berlin in November 1890:

> ". . . as I have never had personal ambitions, since the simple things of life have always been most pleasant to me, it is possible that I should have remained in Southsea permanently but for this new episode in my life"

but I think we may take leave to doubt this. The simple things in life are what we all want — a comfortable home, a contented family, a well-respected position, personal transport, money in the bank — but these things are all relative. Conan Doyle would never have been content to remain a GP at Bush Villa. Even in Southsea there was far too much evidence around him of the better things that men could achieve by work, and influence. Not that one would suggest that he was an envious type; far from it, but he was nothing if not a competitor. Not for him a case of keeping up with the Joneses. He would prefer to have the Joneses try to keep up with him. Like his creation Sherlock Holmes, he liked to come out top, and had every intention of doing so. "Feeling large thoughts rise within me" describes his state of mind on many more occasions that just at the start of *Micah Clarke*. He had his secure anchor in Louise and their daughter. He had the constant encouragement and faith of his mother and, with memories of their humble beginnings in Edinburgh never far from his mind, the urge was strong within himself to do well for the sake of her and his sisters. He knew he was on an upward track, and had the determination to keep on climbing.

For the time being his thoughts of advancement still centred firmly upon his profession. Specialise, that was the answer. Already, in a much-quoted letter to his sister Lottie, he had written of his ideas in this direction:

> "I should go to London and study the eye. I should then go to Berlin and study the eye. I should then go to Paris and study the eye. Having learned all there is to know about the eye, I should come back to London and start as an eye surgeon, still, of course, keeping literature as my milch-cow".

But first, there was more immediate work to be finished. In the intervals of seeing to his patients he must carry on doing what he knew best, driving away at the adventures of his band of heroes, the White Company of English knights with their squires and their archers. It was going to be a long haul, but his recent successes had reinforced his confidence, and he knew he had it in him. Unlike some of us, he didn't have to search for the words. "I cultivate a simple style and avoid long words as far as possible" — it was just a matter of time. And effort. He would have to force himself to decline invitations to play bowls, take tea with the Fords, or indulge in other pleasant ways of passing the time. He had no time to pass the time.

On Wednesday 29 January members of the Portsmouth Cricket Club gathered for their annual meeting, in the Albany Hotel as usual. There was getting to be quite a Service touch about the side these days, what with Captain Lipscomb in the chair, and Major Bethune and C.S.M. Jeffkins on the Committee. Of the original Committee names only that of Dr Conan Doyle remained, and now, after five years, he was to lose his appointment as Captain: Lothian Bonham-Carter got the job. Whether Dr Doyle stepped down voluntarily through pressure of his other commitments, whether his absence in the New Forest was held responsible for the lack of games last summer, whether it was Bonham-Carter's undoubted superiority as a batsman or his social connections which won the day — all these are questions which were confidential to the meeting. Certainly there seems to have been no animosity about the change, for both Doyle and Bonham-Carter played for the United Services as well as Portsmouth later that summer.

Sad to say, Dr Doyle had also lost his regular place in the football team that season. Seddon was still Captain, but the two first choice backs were Pughe and Drew, and Garrington of the Grammar School played as reserve goalkeeper. But he remained a keen supporter. In the first round of the Portsmouth Cup, when Portsmouth defeated the King's Own Yorkshire Light Infantry 1-0 at Gosport, Dr Doyle acted as umpire (i.e. linesman) for his team. It was always useful for a team to supply one of the officials itself, for disputes were not exactly unknown, especially in Cup matches. The *Evening News*, in reporting the final of the Portsmouth Cup between Fremantle and Geneva Cross on 17 March, remarked primly that:

> "although play was slow at times, it is gratifying to note that the contest passed off without any of that roughness which has characterised some of the previous finals".

Portsmouth were knocked out in the second round when they lost 3-0 away to Cowes on 21 December. They fielded a side much weakened by the absence of two players through injury, and three others, including Dr Doyle, who could not make the trip to the Isle of Wight. The difficulties of meeting away-match commitments were illustrated again on 28 December, when Portsmouth met the holders, Royal Engineers, in the second round of the Hampshire Cup at Aldershot. Despite being a depleted side they put up a splendidly contested game but lost by 2 goals to 3. Many men worked six days a week, and neither Pughe nor Drew could get off in time to make the fifty-mile trip, even on a Saturday. You could not simply get in the car and drive there, any more than you could hire a motor-coach for the team. All travel outside the town was by train: one hour by the London train to Guildford, a wait for the connection to Aldershot, then a walk to the ground — a two and a half hours' journey at least. Fortunately Dr Doyle had travelled with his kit, as umpire again, and was able to play, but they were still two men short until a missing forward turned up by a later train.

Dr Doyle was now being reported under his own name, "A.C. Smith" having disappeared for good. In fact he was lucky to be able to get away at all, for throughout January and February all the doctors' surgeries were busy. It was a wet rather than a cold winter. Such games as were played took place in miserable conditions, on grounds made slippery by the constant downpours. In the seasonal gales Broad Street was again flooded, and trains to Hayling Island had to be suspended because of damage to the bridge. Then Hampshire was hit by an influenza epidemic. The *Evening News* reported on 25 January that the prevalence of colds and flu was responsible for an almost total breakdown of Saturday football. Bournemouth, Winchester, Fareham and Southampton as well as Portsmouth were all affected. The Friendly Societies — the Buffaloes, the Foresters and the rest, whose members paid their penny-a-week subscriptions to their health clubs, found that their doctors could hardly cope with the numbers of sick. Even the troopship *Orontes* (the same real ship which brought the fictional Dr Watson back to Portsmouth from India in 1880), homeward bound from Malta, had so many cases on board that she had to borrow a Naval doctor to help out her own hard-pressed medical staff. A Mr James Mackel Lane, aged 29, was found dead in the road near his home in Plymouth Street, Landport. Dr Mulcahy, giving evidence at the inquest on 28 January, fell back on the old formula and stated that death was due to syncope (i.e. failure of the heart's action), brought on by pneumonia which itself had been originated by influenza.

Dr Doyle himself was required to attend an inquest on 20 February. Mrs Mary Ann Boyce, the wife of a tailor, had died in her home at 23 Silver Street. It was stated, somewhat piquantly, that she had not been medically attended for sixteen years, the last time having been for fright — though unfortunately the details of this interesting instance were not given. One evening, sitting in her parlour reading the newspaper, she had complained of pains in the chest, gone upstairs, then fallen unconscious on the floor before she had been able to get into bed. Dr Conan Doyle had been sent for, but had to pronounce that life was extinct. He duly confirmed that death was due to syncope, the result of natural causes.

In all probability it was professional calls of this kind which prevented Dr Doyle from keeping up his record of hundred per cent attendances at the Literary Society's Tuesday lectures. He and Louise had been to hear General Drayson on "The Art of Killing" on 3 December, but he had had to miss the next two, including Dr Nathan Raw, Medical Officer at the Lunatic Asylum, on "Memory and How to improve it". General Drayson's talk, despite its grim title, turned out to be a fairly light-hearted survey of primitive hunting weapons: the sling, the bow and arrow (more efficient than the musket, he said), the assegai, blowpipe and poisoned dart, and so on. It gave the General the opportunity to demonstrate the action of a boomerang (what a pity we have no description of this enlivening interlude), and Dr Doyle the chance to relate a tale of his own attempt at gun-running. On his West African voyage he had tried to sell a number of old Birmingham rifles to the natives, only to find that the chiefs were already well equipped with modern Winchesters and Remingtons. All he succeeded in doing was to barter one rifle for a toothbrush, ho-ho.

On 4 February a Naval surgeon, Dr Gilbert Kirker, delivered what the newspapers called "an exhaustive paper" entitled "Sanitary Notes on Egypt and Palestine". Plagues, epidemics, water supplies — they were among foreign drains for a change. It was at this meeting that Percy Boulnois had to announce his resignation from the Presidency of the Society. After seven years in charge of the drains in Portsmouth he had managed to land the prestige appointment of City Engineer at Liverpool, and he was to leave Portsmouth very shortly.

Only thirty people turned up to hear Dr Norris on "Vital Statistics" on 18 March (no doubt there would have been a great many more had the title had its present-day significance). It gave Dr Ward Cousins the chance to remind his listeners of the need for decent ventilation and proper drainage in housing construction, and provoked a long editorial in the Hampshire Post deploring the lack of intellectual aspiration among the town's people:

> "Simultaneously with the falling off in audiences at the Guildhall, Mr Boughton at the Theatre Royal has been rewarded with crowded houses".

Perhaps because of this — or more likely, perhaps not — no fewer than one hundred and twenty people, including Dr and Mrs Conan Doyle, turned out for the last lecture of the season: Dr D. Nicholson on "Witches and Witchcraft". In a witty and entertaining talk Dr Nicholson, a former member of the Society who had since removed to Scotland, described in detail the rituals and superstitions of both classical and mediaeval witches, and the crude and unjust methods of the authorities in dealing with them. King James, he said, who was a great authority on the subject, had computed that for every male witch or wizard in the world there were at least twenty female ones. This was because the Devil had got on so well with Eve that he had been friendly with the ladies ever since. He ended on a serious note by counselling his listeners against dwelling too much on the supernatural, which, within his own experience, had been the wreck of many an otherwise excellent intellect.

It was a warning which was lost on at least one member of his audience. Dr Conan Doyle rose to propose the vote of thanks, with memories of Milo de Meyer's demonstration of the previous year still fresh in his mind. He was certainly not disposed to treat such a subject with flippancy. Wherever there was a belief extending over many countries for a long period of time, he insisted, there generally was some substance of truth in it. What about the experiments being conducted by Professor Charcot and others in Paris, on mesmerism and clairvoyance? A person, when under trance, had been given a piece of sugar and told:

> "This is arsenic. In three months time you will administer this to your dearest friend".

On awaking the man knew nothing about the matter; but three months afterwards, while under overpowering influence, he did administer the sugar as he had been told. Surely this was a case of preternatural power being used for malevolent purposes. Nobody could read of such work being undertaken by eminent scientists, without taking it seriously.

Percy Boulnois was leaving. Earlier in the year he had been chosen as the next President of the Association of Muncipal and Sanitary Engineers, and the time had come for him to take up his new post at Liverpool. Dr Doyle took it upon himself to organise a small committee with the object of presenting a suitable testimonial to mark the departure of his friend. He appointed himself a secretary and

A corner of the Canoe Lake, Southsea, which was constructed on waste ground in 1886 to the design of Percy Boulnois, the Borough Engineer. (Photo: R.F. Reynolds, Cosham).

treasurer, and led the way with a subscription of one guinea. At the end of February a nice little party was held at the Grosvenor Hotel (he didn't know it then, but ten months later he was to be the guest of honour at a similar function himself). General Drayson took the chair. The Mayor (Mr Ellis), the ex-Mayor (Mr Addison), Dr Vernon Ford, Headmaster Jerrard, Hugh MacLaughlan and other friends of the Literary Society were there with their ladies, together with Mr Thomas Cousins, Clerk to the Magistrates. Champagne was served. General Drayson made a nice little speech of farewell. Mr Cousins offered a vote of thanks to Dr Doyle and his committee, and suitable replies were returned. Mr Boulnois was presented with a gold watch and chain, and his wife received a most handsome clock measuring two feet long by eighteen inches high. It was made in white marble with bronze gilt mounts, bearing a pair of allegorical figures representing the Engineer's two great enemies, earth and water, with the third enemy, time, beneath. Both items were supplied by the well-known jewellers Messrs Ezekiel Emanuel, of the Hard, Portsea.

Much of Boulnois's work for the town during his seven years as Borough Engineer having perforce been underground, there is little enough now to remind us of his presence, but he did leave one visible representation of his work. The Canoe Lake at Craneswater near the

South Parade Pier, a popular venue for children's boating, model yacht racing, and (occasionally) swan feeding, which was created out of a piece of waste land in 1886, was built to his design. His main task had been to supervise the construction of Portsmouth's first comprehensive drainage and sewerage system — the need for which, in such a low-lying town with a steadily increasing population, had been a constant preoccupation of the Corporation. The pumping station at Eastney, in which two splendid old beam engines built by James Watt can still be seen in working order, has been preserved as a museum.

The Council of the Literary Society met at Riversdale, Dr Ward Cousin's home, at the end of April and nominated Dr James Watson as their President for the next season. No mention was made of Dr Conan Doyle, it being assumed that he would continue as usual in his role of joint Secretary.

A few contemporary items from the *Portsmouth Times*:

"22 February. The Phonograph or Talking Machine. Mr Edison's marvellous invention will be exhibited and described by Mr W. Lynd MIEE FRMS at the Portland Hall on Monday next at 8 pm and on Tuesday at 3 pm, with illustrations represented by the very latest machine, which arrived in England only two months ago. Human voices and music, songs, selections by brass bands and solos on various musical instruments will be reproduced with outstanding accuracy".

"22 February. SHOCKING SCENE AT AN EXECUTION. Three murderers were hanged on Thursday — two men named Schloop and Cole at Philadelphia, and another named Hopkins at Bellefonte, Pa. A shocking scene was enacted at the execution of the man Hopkins, who had been found guilty of murdering his wife and mother-in-law. The rope broke and the prisoner was picked up insensible. A fresh rope was, however, brought and the second time the execution was effectively performed".

Did they wake him up before they hanged him again?

"29 March. STARVED TO DEATH. Liverpool. At the Assizes before Justice Mathew, William Pearson aged 51, labourer, of Southport, and Eliza, aged 38, his wife, who were last night found guilty of the manslaughter of two illegitimate children who were placed in their care, were brought up for sentence. Mrs Bray (or Oldfield), mother of the children, was acquitted. It was alleged that both children died of starvation. *They were insured.* William Pearson was sentenced to seven years penal servitude, and Eliza to five years".

"26 April. An American girl has started riding astride in New York. She is said to be a graceful horsewoman, and to look well in her peculiar habilments, which consist of a habit for each leg. The division of cloth between the two is nobly impartial, and the skirts hang down over the stirrups. The bodice is the orthodox, gentlemanly, neat, trim garment to which we are all accustomed, and the undergear consists of riding breeches and top boots. One fails to see how a woman can stick on properly in this position. . ."

The Sign Of Four came out in Lippincott's Magazine in February, without making any noticeable impact on the Portsmouth newspapers (one individual upon whom it did make an impact was the Philadelphia tobacconist, who is said to have wanted to know where he could obtain a copy of Sherlock Holmes's monograph on 140 different kinds of tobacco ash). Then in March Messrs Longmans, no doubt persuaded by the success of *Micah Clarke*, brought out a book containing ten of Conan Doyle's magazine short stories, selected by himself, under the title *The Captain of the Pole-Star*. It is an interesting volume, not least for its dedication:

> "To my friend Major-General A.W. Drayson, as a slight token of my admiration for his great and as yet unrecognised services to Astronomy"

(and still unrecognised, we fear). Besides the title story it contains three more of his tales of the occult: *The Man From Archangel*, *John Barrington Cowles*, and *The Ring of Thoth*; his early success, *J. Habakuk Jephson's Statement*; one spoof mystery, *That Little Square Box*; one pseudo-scientific fantasy, *The Great Keinplatz Experiment* (German scholars will easily recognise the simple leg-pull in the place-name); one sentimental tale, *John Huxford's Hiatus*; one rough adventure, *The Parson of Jackman's Gulch*; and the elementary satire, *A Literary Mosaic*. The whole provides a perfect example of the author's range and versatility, even in the apprentice years of his writing career. Any one of these tales offers a splendid, fast-moving read even now, if you can bear to switch off your television set for ten minutes or so.

In at least one of them we have another example of how, as in *The Sign of Four* (and not a few of the other Sherlock Holmes adventures) the author can become so carried away by his theme that little inconsistencies of detail escape his notice. *John Huxford's Hiatus* begins in a little west-country fishing town, not even thinly disguised as Brisport, where the owner of a cork-making factory has been forced to close down owing to competition from cheap foreign imports (not a new idea for a tale, nor yet an out-of-date one):

> "It was a murky, foggy Saturday afternoon in November when the hands were paid for the last time"

writes the narrator, and then, hey presto, a couple of paragraphs later, "they began to flock out into the sunlight". Many years later, rich, famous, and brimming with self-confidence, Dr Doyle had his own answer to trivial criticisms of this kind. In a railway story he had a passenger escaping from his compartment by going out of the offside door and climbing into another train running on a parallel track alongside. It was pointed out to him that at the place designated there was only a single track, not two. "So what?" he replied grandly (or words to that effect), "I make another line". For the highest-paid short story writer of his time, that was good enough.

The Captain of The Pole-Star collection was published at six shillings. The first printing, rather cautiously limited to 750 copies, was sold out on the day of publication, and a second printing followed rapidly. Royalties were coming in at a satisfactory rate. Then in April Chatto and Windus brought out *The Firm of Girdlestone*, also at six shillings, but this too seems to have been overlooked by the Portsmouth reviewers. A couple of months later, however, the *Hampshire Telegraph* did have a special offering for its readers. "Coming next week" said the announcement in its issue of 28 June:

> "A New Novel, THE SIGN OF FOUR, by A. CONAN DOYLE. 'The Sign of Four' is the latest work of the brilliant novelist, Dr A. Conan Doyle, whose first great work 'Micah Clarke' now ranks with 'Lorna Doone' and 'Westward Ho!' as one of the three most powerful historical novels of this generation. 'The Sign of Four' is the exciting and fascinating history of a crime. It is rich in novel characters and abounds in ingenious situations. The scene is laid partly among the convicts of the Andaman Islands and partly in London".

So, the author is already 'the brilliant novelist', no longer just 'the Southsea doctor'. It must have gratified him to observe that his reputation was founded upon *Micah Clarke*, whereas today we are astonished to note that the *Telegraph* did not think fit to mention the names of either Holmes or Watson in its advance publicity for *The Sign Of Four*. Evidently, even in Portsmouth, they were far from being household names then.

Meanwhile the author, shutting his eyes to the July sunshine, climbed the stairs once more to his little room, fitted himself into his creaking writing chair, which ever seemed to be getting too small for him, cleared a space on his littered desk, and got on with his self-imposed task. No question of watching for an accident in the road outside now. In fact, if there was one he rather hoped that Claremont or one of the others would be there first to see to it. He was over the hump and on to the final chapters, but that only made it harder to keep pushing it along. It had been a long book, longer than *Micah Clarke*, and he always said afterwards that *The White Company* was above all the one he had most enjoyed writing; but not even Louise, who kept him plied with cups of cocoa while he was writing, could properly appreciate the effort that it had been.

Not that any of this comes through in the work itself. *The White Company* is a straightforward, episodic sequence of adventurous encounters with no deep plot, well suited to serialisation, though the author may have denied that that is what he had in mind. There is rather a lot of the "By St Paul", "By my hilt", "By the twang of my bowstring" type of dialogue, but such is the pace and vigour of the writing that you are carried irresistibly onwards, skipping over the archaic conversations and the foreign words without a thought of bothering to look them up. You can feel the author's relish in his battle scenes:

> "At the very foot of the stair, close to the open door of their chamber, lay the Seneschal and his wife; she with her head shorn from her shoulders, he thrust through with a sharpened stake, which still protruded from either side of his body. Three servants of the castle lay dead beside them, all torn and draggled, as if a pack of wolves had been upon them. In front of the central guest-chamber stood Du Guesclin and Sir Nigel, half-clad and unarmoured, with the mad joy of battle gleaming in their eyes. Their heads were thrown back, their lips compressed, their blood-stained swords poised over their right shoulders, and their left feet thrown out. Three dead men lay huddled together in front of them; while a fourth, with the blood spurting from a severed vessel, lay back with updrawn knees, breathing in wheezy gasps. Further back — all panting together like the wind in a tree — there stood a group of fierce wild creatures, bare-armed and bare-legged, gaunt, unshaven, with deep-set murderous eyes and wild-beast faces. With their flashing teeth, their bristling hair, their mad leapings and screamings, they seemed to Alleyne more like fiends from the pit than men of flesh and blood. Even as he looked, they broke into a hoarse yell and dashed once more upon the two knights, hurling themselves madly upon their sword-points; clutching, scrambling, biting, tearing, careless of wounds if they could but drag the two soldiers to earth. . ."

There are tournaments, duels, sea fights, land fights, fist fights. There is an impromptu archery contest which is as good as anything dreamed up by a Robin Hood or cowboy romancer. There is the occult, too. The Lady Tiphaine, a clairvoyant Frenchwoman, is credited with foretelling the rise of the British Empire (but not, naturally enough, its subsequent decline):

> "The lady sat with parched lips, and her breath came quick and fast.

'My God!' she cried, 'What is this that is shown me? Whence come they, these peoples, these lordly nations, these mighty countries which rise up before me? I look beyond, and others rise, and yet others, far and farther to the shores of the uttermost waters. They crowd! They swarm! The world is given to them, and it resounds with the clang of their hammers and the ringing of their church bells. They call them many names, and they rule them this way or that, but they are all English, for I can hear the voices of the people. On I go, and onwards over seas where man hath never yet sailed, and I see a great land under new stars and a strange sky, and still the land is England. Where have her children not gone? What have they not done? Her banner is planted on ice. Her banner is scorched in the sun. She lives athwart the lands, and her shadow is over the seas. Bertrand, Bertrand! We are undone, for the buds of her bud are even as our choicest flower!' Her voice rose into a wild cry, and throwing up her arms she sank back white and nerveless into the deep oaken chair.

'It is over,' said Du Guesclin moodily, as he raised her drooping head with his strong brown hand. 'Wine for the lady, Squire! The blessed hour of sight has passed!' "

Eventually it was all done, and early in July Dr Doyle wrote the last few words of his most ambitious work to date. Eighteen months it had taken him, from conception to completion, in sharp contrast to the speed with which he had been able to turn out his two Sherlock Holmes books. No wonder he threw away his pen and splashed ink all down his wife's wallpaper in celebration. Thankfully he parcelled up the manuscript and sent it off to James Payn, his usual first port of call with a new work. Even more thankfully he learned that Payn (who had rejected *Micah Clarke*) had accepted it for serialisation in *The Cornhill*. In a few weeks the contract was settled: £200 for the serial, probably starting early next year, and a further £350 for the book rights. Well, it was certainly better than doctoring; but could he keep it up, and bring up a family on an author's shaky earnings?

At least he could allow himself his Saturday cricket again. He played for Portsmouth in the first two rounds of the Hampshire Cup, and several times for the United Services. He even had the satisfaction of getting the wickets of both Bonham-Carter and Bethune in a match against the Corinthians, but strained his back so badly in the process that he had to give up playing for the rest of the season.

The big civic event of the year was the official opening of the new Guildhall on 7 August by the Prince of Wales (the future King Edward VII). William Pink, now an Alderman, was Mayor for the fifth time, and duly received a knighthood to mark the occasion. All the papers published double-page spreads of the event, with pen-and-ink sketches

Portsmouth Guildhall, officially opened by the Prince of Wales (later King Edward VII) on 7 August, 1890. The building was bombed and gutted by fire in the war but now stands again substantially as Conan Doyle knew it, except for the cupola and the small domed cappings over the corners.

of the building, portraits of the Royal pair, bearded Councillors, the Contractors and other personalities involved. In the great air raid of January 1941 the building was hit by many incendiaries. It was a night of a particularly low tide; water was scarce, and there were so many fires raging in other parts of the city that nothing could be done to save the Guildhall. The inside was completely gutted, but the shell remained intact. Now, with the interior restored to its proper dignity and usefulness and incorporating a fine concert hall, it is still able to present the same outward appearance that Dr Conan Doyle knew.

There may well have been something of a temporary vacuum in his intellectual life after the completion of *The White Company*, but if there was any reaction it does not seem to have set in until a month or two later. In September Blackwoods of Edinburgh published his short story *A Physiologist's Wife*, and in December *The Surgeon of Gaster Fell*, a tale set on the bare Pennine moors above Masongill and probably inspired by the afflictions of his father, came out in *Chambers' Journal* — but both of these were probably written at some time earlier. Life at Bush Villa carried on as normal. On 24 September he presided over the annual meeting of the Portsmouth Football Club at the Albany. Seddon, "whose loss would be severely felt", had gone, and A.H. Wood was unanimously elected Captain in his place. On 25 October the Council of the Literary Society again accepted the hospitality of Bush Villa for their pre-season meeting.

Dr Watson, as President, gave his opening address to the Society on 4 November. At last it seemed that they had a proper home; over two hundred members and guests met, by kind permission of the Town Council, in the Grand Jury Room of the new Guildhall. Dr Watson spoke on Technical Education; a solid and thoughtful lecture, making clear his ideas on the distinction between technical and general education and putting the case for some practical recognition of these differences in the British educational system. Lack of proper technical education led to too much division of labour, encouraged restrictive practices in the Trade Unions, and rendered Britain at a disadvantage in the face of competition from the Continent. He emphasised, however, that technical education should always be left in the care of local authorities, because they would be able to appraise local needs and not spend money unnecessarily.

General Drayson, like many of those present, found much to agree with in Dr Watson's address. He was all against the Unions:

> "England would never maintain her supremacy if the principle of eight hours work, eight hours recreation, and eight hours sleep were adopted, for if the people on the Continent were content to work twelve hours a day they would beat the Englishman out of the field"

grumbled the old soldier.

Dr and Mrs Doyle were present as usual, though he did not make any comment. Perhaps it was now that a reaction from literature back to medicine set in, for he suddenly conceived the idea to go to Berlin to witness Robert Koch's demonstration of his supposed cure for tuberculosis. "I could give no clear reason for this, but it was an irresistible impulse and I at once determined to go". Perhaps, as suggested by Rodin and Key, it was Koch's article in the *British Medical Journal* of 15 November that suddenly focussed his mind back on to medical matters again. He must have gone off at very short notice indeed (he probably got his copy of the *British Medical Journal* a day or two in advance of the published date), leaving Portsmouth early on the Saturday and crossing via Dover in time to catch the overnight express to arrive in Berlin on the morning of Sunday, the 16th. Once there he found that, not having booked a seat, he could not get in to the demonstration lecture, but he was able to see some of Koch's "guinea-pig" patients in the local hospital wards. In less than a couple of days he had made up his mind, and already on Monday evening he sat down to write a long letter to the London *Daily Telegraph* advising caution over Koch's claims. He was going to be the one who would be first with the message. After all, he was not just any old provincial GP any more.

Third Ordinary Meeting
18th Dec: 1890

The Third Ordinary meeting of the Portsmouth Literary and Scientific Society was held at the Grand Jury Room, Town Hall, on Thursday evening the 18th December 1890.

The chair was occupied by the President (Dr. J. Watson) and about 40 ladies and gentlemen were present.

The minutes of the last meeting were read and confirmed.

Mr. Alfred A. Seale read a paper entitled: "An hour with Robert Browning."

A discussion followed, in which the chairman (Dr. J. Watson), General. A. W. Drayson, and Mr. J. Hay took part.

A unanimous vote of thanks terminated the proceedings.

James Watson —

Copy of a page of the Minutes of the Portsmouth Literary and Scientific Society, signed by Dr Watson during his year of office as President of the Society.

He was Dr Conan Doyle, the brilliant novelist. His name was known. His letter was published on 20 November, and he was back in Portsmouth by the weekend.

The Berlin trip, and particularly a discussion he had had with an English doctor, Malcolm Morris, on the train had rekindled his earlier somewhat vague ideas about setting himself up as an eye specialist in London. Now his mind was made up. A somewhat bemused Louise was told that they would be leaving Bush Villa before Christmas, and going to Vienna. What, in the middle of winter? Why of course. It would be just right for skating. On the afternoon of 2 December, the day of their next lecture, the Council of the Literary Society went into emergency session. Dr Claremont was elected as the new joint Secretary, and it was decided to invite a few members to take part in a friendly dinner to mark the forthcoming departure of Dr Conan Doyle.

The dinner was held on 13 December, in the Grosvenor Hotel at the end of Western Parade. Thirty-four gentlemen (sad to say, no ladies) were present besides the guest of honour. Dr Watson took the chair, with Dr Doyle on his right and Alderman Pink on his left. Dr Ward Cousins, Drs Claremont, Axford, Mumby, Raw and a couple of others were there; Generals Drayson and Harward; Captain Jackson and another naval Captain; Albert Addison, a former Mayor; John

A rare picture showing the Grosvenor Hotel at the corner of Western Parade, Southsea. Conan Doyle and Percy Boulnois were dined out on separate occasions at the Grosvenor. Southsea Terrace can be seen on the far side of the Common. The hotel has since been converted into flats.

Brickwood, A.E. Cogswell, A.W. White; James Graham Niven, elderly and white-bearded, a name we have not come across before (he was the founder and owner of the *Hampshire Telegraph* and *Evening News*), with of course his Editor Hugh MacLaughlan; J.W. Boughton, manager of the Theatre Royal; A.H. Wood, W.E. Grant and Lancelot Pares from the Football Club; and one or two cricketers — though none of his early friends of the old North End Club can be identified.

After the fashion of the times, there was a long list of toasts. Dr Watson led off with the Queen. Mr Addison proposed The Services, and General Harward and Captain Jackson replied in order of seniority. General Drayson then rose to drink the health of their guest. Speaking from a soldier's experience in various quarters of the world, he declared Dr Conan Doyle to be intellectually, physically and socially one of the most admirable companions he had ever met (Hear, hear). He would leave Southsea having established a name there that would ever remain in the memories of all present; and not only that, but his name was known wherever the English language was spoken. Although he, General Drayson, knew that Dr Cousins did not believe in phrenology, yet, whether they believed it or not, there was in Dr Doyle's head an extraordinary bump of observation.

Dr Doyle replied with suitable thanks, and amused the company with the story of his punch-up, in top-hat and frock-coat, with the bully on his very first evening in the town. Mr Niven toasted the Mayor, and paid tribute to his work as long-standing Chairman of the Sanitary and Drainage Committee. Dr Axford toasted the President, and Dr Watson in reply looked forward to the time when Dr Doyle would be the guest of a far more august assembly than the present one. Mr MacLaughlan toasted the Visitors, and Alfred Wood replied on behalf of the sportsmen. Mr Hay toasted the Ladies and, there not being any, Dr Raw responded. Dr Doyle interpolated the health of Dr Cousins, General Drayson toasted the Press, and that was the end of the list.

It was a nice send-off — though not perhaps quite as good as the one Dr Doyle himself had organised for Percy Boulnois. No marble clock for Louise, or anything like that. Well, he had given them pretty short notice. Perhaps Dr Watson felt, after due consideration, that such a presentation might be an unnecessary extravagance in view of the seeming impermanence of their future domestic arrangements.

At home, Dr Doyle was already clearing up. Old patients came to say goodbye, and those who were still on the treatment list were handed over to Dr Claremont. Little Mary Louise, now nearly four, was put into the care of Mrs Hawkins who was now living in the Isle of Wight. The furniture was put into store, and Bush Villa was closed down. Thus did Conan Doyle's one and only general practice fade away. For a couple of days he and his wife took a room at "Charlmont", Mrs Harries's apartment house at 12, Western Parade. Last minute arrangements had been made for them to spend Christmas at Masongill, after first breaking the journey north by calling on Dr and Mrs Hoare at Birmingham. Shortly after the 15th they got into a cab for the station, and so shook the dust of Southsea — or rather the snow, for it was that sort of a day — from their feet.

But not quite for ever.

CHAPTER **X**

1896 - The Old Boy

IN 1896, six and a half years after he left the town, Conan Doyle came back to Southsea. On Saturday 16 May, the *Portsmouth Times* carried a report of a cricket match between Hampshire Rovers and the Army Service Corps, played the previous Thursday in fine weather:

> "Rovers had the start in batting, and runs were quickly made. Dr Conan Doyle, who is staying in the town for six weeks after his trip to Egypt, joined partnership with Pillans, and showed some good cricket. Though he was disposed of before lunch, 36 of the 71 shown on the 'telegraph' were registered in his name".

On another page the paper drew attention to his new serial on bare-fist fighting in Regency times, *Rodney Stone*, then running in the *Strand Magazine*:

> "We think this historical romance will have a reputation as great as 'Micah Clarke' ".

A fortnight later the same paper included two more references to the doctor, both of them slightly inaccurate in detail. The first, in a column headed Jottings, read:

> "Dr Conan Doyle intends spending several months in Southsea, and in the intervals of relaxation from writing a novel, to be published in the autumn, he is polishing up his cricketing talent".

In fact his stay was to be measured in weeks, not months, as was indicated in the earlier notice. The novel he was working on was *Uncle Bernac*, a tale of Napoleonic times which had been giving him some trouble. It was one of those stories which start out with a good idea and then seem to run out of steam half way through; though he did manage to finish it in due course, he freely admitted afterwards that he was never satisfied with it.

The other reference again related to cricket:

> "Before Dr Doyle gained literary laurels good scores were frequently appended to the name 'A.C. Smith', and this week, on the

United Services ground and at Winchester, he showed that he could still wield the willow with considerable effect".

We know of course that 'Smith' was just Dr Doyle's footballing alias, cricket being a gentlemen's game requiring no disguises, but in other respects the report was correct enough. Playing for Hampshire Rovers again in a two-day match against United Services he had scored no less than 84 not out and taken two wickets.

Conan Doyle's biographers, without exception, have completely ignored this little interlude in his life. This is a pity since apart from illustrating his continued affection for the town in which his career began, it also uncovers two little Sherlockian mysteries whose solution we can now only guess at.

The Portsmouth which greeted him when he stepped off the train at the Town Station would look very much the same as that which he had left. True, building was going on as the town gradually spread itself eastwards in the direction of Copnor and Eastney, but this would not be apparent to the visitor, and Southsea itself would be just as he had known it. Elm Grove was still a leafy avenue of private villas. Horse trams still plied the streets; powers to electrify the system were being sought, and the Corporation was thinking of taking the whole enterprise over, but neither of these changes came into effect until the year 1900. A.W. White meanwhile was toying with the idea, once the Corporation had bought him out, of laying down a light railway to run electric trams from Cosham out into the country as far as Horndean, but this too was still a few years in the future.

Bush Villa was now occupied by a Miss H.M. Lawrence, a dressmaker, and a bay window had been built on to the front of his old consulting room to serve as a showplace for her wares. Sadly, Dr Pike had been "removed by death", carried off by cancer at the tragically early age of 42 in April 1891. Dr Watson had attended him, but the condition was inoperable. Most of their old Literary Society colleagues were still in being. Dr Claremont continued as Secretary. General Drayson was still in residence at 20 Ashburton Road, ever ready to blind an audience with some more of his astronomical science. General Cox remained at 26 South Parade. General Harward had removed from Kingston Crescent into Southsea, at 15 Merton Road.

Dr Vernon Ford was still combining his work at the Eye and Ear Infirmary with running his private practice. He too had moved into Southsea, at first to Shaftesbury Road, but for the past three years he had been installed with his family in South View Lodge, a handsomely proportioned large villa at 53 Kent Road, on the north side close to St Jude's Church. This house was one of a pair built about 1844 by Thomas Owen. Though semi-detached the two do not quite match, in typical Owen fashion, and fortunately both have survived the war and

General view of part of Highland Road Cemetery. The holly bush marks the grave of Dr Pike, Conan Doyle's friend and neighbour, who died in 1891.

other developments. The neighbour, No. 51, was occupied by Charles Plumley Childe, another surgeon.

Dr Watson, still happily settled in "Elmwood", had been appointed Honorary Physician at the Royal Hospital in the vacancy left by the death of Dr Pike. In December 1892 *The Lancet* had published a letter from him describing an operation on a child's liver which he and Dr Cousins had undertaken there. At the annual meeting of the British Medical Association (southern branch) held in Portsmouth in 1896 he took the chair, and delivered an address on Chinese Medicine. Dr Cousins himself, like Dr Doyle, had been struck down by a near-fatal attack of influenza in January 1892; his wife had died, but happily he had recovered and was now a JP and the new President of the British Medical Association. George Evatt, the Army doctor on the staff of Netley hospital who had been a popular guest lecturer at the Literary Society, was being posted to Hong Kong as Principal Medical Officer with the rank of Surgeon-Lieutenant-Colonel. There he was to relieve Surgeon-Colonel A.F. Preston, who had been ordered home pending his promotion to Major-General. Preston, then a Surgeon-Major, had been severely wounded while serving with the 66th Regiment, the Berkshires, at the Battle of Maiwand in Afghanistan on 27 July 1880. Readers of *A Study in Scarlet* may remember that this was exactly the fate which caused the fictional Dr Watson to be invalided home and led to his first meeting with Sherlock Holmes in the chemical laboratory of St Bartholomew's Hospital. Any resemblance between the early careers of these two doctors may not be entirely coincidental.

Norman Pares had left the Grammar School to become Rector of Horsell, Woking. The Reverend Shutte had died, but Lindsay Young was still in charge at St John's with over thirty years of his ministry yet to run. A new Vicar had been appointed to St Mary's, Portsea. This fine church, the third to stand on the site, had been consecrated in 1889; it was not until after he died in 1891 that it was revealed that most of the money for its construction had been given by W.H. Smith, of the chain of bookselling and stationery stores. The new Vicar was the Reverend Cosmo Gordon Lang, one of a number of distinguished incumbents of St Mary's. His predecessor, Edgar Jacob, became Bishop of Newcastle. Lang himself went on to become Bishop of Stepney, Archbishop of York and then of Canterbury. A successor was Cyril Garbett, an old boy of Portsmouth Grammar School, who also became Archbishop of York. At the same time as Lang was appointed one of the curates, the Reverend Henry Lafone, left to become Vicar of Ambleside and later Archdeacon of Westmorland. In 1907 it was this same Henry Lafone who married Dr James Watson's only daughter Margaret.

All these promotions, however, were as nothing compared with the transformation which had taken place in Dr Conan Doyle's affairs in the intervening years. He had achieved reasonable success as a general practitioner in Southsea, but his attempt to become an eye specialist in London had failed; in less than a couple of months he had abandoned it in favour of becoming a full time writer. After spending Christmas 1890 with his mother and family at Masongill he had cheerfully taken Louise off to Vienna without having any really organised plan of what course of study he ought to take there. Even then he already had the contract for another book in his pocket. Harmsworth the newspaper publisher wanted a serial for his weekly paper *Answers to Correspondents*. "My present scale is £5 per thousand words", replied the author, confidently demanding twice the figure he had got for *The Sign of Four* the year before. He started writing it the day after his arrival in Vienna and finished it in just over a fortnight: *The Doings of Raffles Haw*, an early essay into science fiction, unimpressive nowadays, about a chemist and would-be philanthropist who finds out how to make untold wealth by transmuting ordinary metals into gold. Still, at 30,000 words it was another £150 to the good for the serial rights alone — more than enough to cover the hotel bills.

What with this, and the freezing weather, and the fact that he didn't know enough German to follow them properly, such lectures as he did manage to attend were not a success. By the end of March, having first taken his wife to Italy for a few days of sightseeing and sunshine, he was back in London without having added any extra qualification to his name. Nothing daunted, he rented a consulting room at 2 Devonshire Place, on the fringe of the fashionable doctors' quarters of Harley Street and Wimpole Street. Here, for a whole month, he sat from ten in the morning to four in the afternoon without seeing a single patient. He seems to have been relieved, if not actually pleased about it:

> "Could better conditions for reflection and work be found? It was ideal, and so long as I was thoroughly unsuccessful in my professional venture there was every chance of improvement in my literary prospects".

It was here, while waiting for his non-existent patients, that he conceived the idea of a series of magazine-length stories, each complete in itself but featuring the same principal characters (the forerunner of countless others, and of today's radio and TV series), and began concocting a succession of plots set around the personalities of Sherlock Holmes and Dr Watson in their cosy lodgings at 221B Baker Street. They were immediately accepted by the *Strand Magazine*, and the first of the adventures entitled *A Scandal in Bohemia* came out in July. By the end of the year six had been published, one every month. The sales of the *Strand* shot up, people queued up at the bookstalls to buy each new issue, and the names of Holmes, Watson and A. Conan Doyle became household words all over the country. And it is the illustrations to these, drawn by Sidney Paget, which first present the received "English" depiction of the Holmes figure and physiognomy. The fourth adventure, *The Boscombe Valley Mystery*, shows Holmes for the first time in his country travelling gear of long tweed coat and deerstalker hat.

In his second month at Devonshire Place Conan Doyle was struck down with a very severe attack of influenza. By the time he recovered from this he had decided that it was a waste of money to pay a high rent just for a room to write in, and he never saw his consulting room again. He found a nice big house at South Norwood, not far from the Crystal Palace, and here for two years he enjoyed a full life of happy domesticity and ever-increasing literary success. Money was now coming in from all directions. The *Strand* paid him £50 each for a further five Holmes adventures, irrespective of length. The whole set of eleven came out in book form as *The Adventures of Sherlock Holmes* — and they have never been out of print since. *The Sign of Four* took off and was selling by the thousand. The *Strand* pleaded for another dozen adventures. He asked for £1000, hoping they might refuse, but was accepted without demur. And not only Sherlock Holmes. Both *Micah Clarke* and *The White Company* were going through edition after edition. Between devising more Holmes plots he wrote another long historical novel, *The Refugees*, set in Paris and North America, and a short one, *The Great Shadow*, about the rise of Napoleon and the Battle of Waterloo. *Beyond The City*, another shortish book, is a genial description of life among their neighbours in suburban London of the nineties.

By now he had enough money coming in to enable his sisters Connie and Lottie to throw up their jobs as governesses and come and share his home. Louise had her second baby, a fine little boy whom they called Alleyne Kingsley, after his hero in *The White Company* and the author Charles Kingsley. When not working he relaxed by socializing among the literary circles of London, playing tennis in the garden, and pedalling around the country roads on his big tricycle, dressed in his gents sporting outfit of knickerbockers, Norfolk jacket and round schoolboy cap, with Louise perched up on a little seat in front catching all the draughts. No traffic problems then, of course; just clouds of dust from the odd passing wagon or trap, and Louise got most of that too. To the big, optimistic, aggressively healthy ex-doctor, life at times must have seemed almost too good to be true.

And so, alas, it was. In November 1893 Louise fell ill. "Galloping consumption", i.e. turberculosis, was confirmed. There was no cure for this fatal disease. Complete rest, and prolonged exposure to clean fresh air, at the seaside or more preferably a high altitude, was all the doctors could advise. Within a matter of days Conan Doyle took his whole family off to Switzerland, with Lottie to look after the baby and leaving Mrs Hawkins in charge of the house. For the next two years, apart from occasional short business trips to London and a highly successful American lecture tour, his life centred around the resort of Davos. Typically, Conan Doyle soon found himself taking a leading part in the local sports, becoming famous as a skater and as the first man to popularise the use of Norwegian skis (then called snow-shoes) in Switzerland. Typically also, he carried on writing, as prolific as ever. *The Stark Munro Letters* dates from this period, as also does *The Parasite*, his dark tale of an evil woman possessed of such hypnotic powers that she is able to induce by remote control not only murder, but passionate love as well, in the mind of her chosen victim. He was finished with Holmes now, or thought he was, having sent both Holmes and Professor Moriarty to their deaths over the Reichenbach Falls in the last of the second set of adventures. Instead he had created another of his larger-than-life characters, the extravagantly dashing and boastful cavalry officer Brigadier Etienne Gerard, possessor at once of the stoutest heart and the thickest head in Napoleon's army. Like Holmes he had a basis in life but was drawn much larger by his author's imagination and inventiveness. *The Adventures of Gerard* duly began their monthly appearances in The *Strand*. They are just as ingeniously contrived as those of Sherlock Holmes, but the Brigadier has never achieved the cult following of the great detective. He did get a racehorse named after him, and it may be a nice point as to whether this is a greater compliment than having a steam locomotive named after you, as Holmes did. A whole clutch of other short stories, including many of Conan Doyle's tales of medical life, also belong to this period.

In May 1895 on one of his visits home Conan Doyle met a fellow-author, Grant Allen, who lived at Hindhead in Surrey. Why go to the trouble and expense of living in Switzerland?, asked this man. Did he not know that the air of the South Downs was just as pure? Fired with the idea, Conan Doyle went down to Hindhead, found an ideal site just below the main road at the top end of the village, and sent down to Portsmouth for his old friend Henry Ball to come and design a house for him. This was to be no Bush Villa, but a gentleman's residence grand enough to arouse the respect of any of the big men in Southsea. Money was no serious object. Already he had his boxing story *Rodney Stone* on the stocks; the *Strand* was paying him £1500 for the serial, and Smith Elder had offered no less than £4000 in advance royalties for the book. He would have his own full size billiard room, a dining room big enough for thirty, other rooms and offices to match. Bedrooms for guests and servants; stabling for horses, not just one, but six; a tennis

court; and a fine glass screen in the front hall to display his family coats of arms. How long would it take? queried the prospective owner eagerly, as if he thought it could be ready next week. Um, said the architect. There would be the detailed drawings to do, quantities to estimate, contracts to let — give him a year, say, to be on the safe side. Very well, then; next May it is. Back to Portsmouth went Ball, well pleased with his commission, and back to Davos went Conan Doyle.

That autumn he took his family to Egypt, to try the winter climate there. They went for a cruise on the Nile, and then, while Louise rested in the sunshine on the balcony of their Cairo hotel her husband went off into the desert on some adventures of his own. He had his photograph taken alongside the Pyramids, sitting

Undershaw, the house which Henry Ball built for Conan Doyle at Hindhead in Surrey. It is now a hotel.

on a donkey which looked several sizes too small for him, made a hazardous overnight trip to an old Coptic monastery, visited the British army in the Sudan and had dinner with General Kitchener. A desert adventure story, *The Tragedy of the Korosko*, and several shorter tales with a military flavour, made their appearance in due time as the practical results of his Middle Eastern experiences.

By the first week of May 1896, as arranged, they were all back in England. To his intense disappointment and annoyance (he had had very little experience with builders), the splended new house at Hindhead was hardly begun. Months and months of work remained to be done before it would be ready for occupation.

It is at this point that another Portsmouth cleric touches on the Conan Doyle story. This was the Reverend Robert Radclyffe Dolling. Father Dolling, as he liked to be known, was of striking appearance, with broad, clean-shaven mobile features strongly reminiscent of the American actor Edward G. Robinson; a powerful personality, a man of fearless, outspoken opinions and seemingly boundless energy. Like Reginald Shutte, he did an immense amount of practical good work at his Winchester College mission in a desperate slum area near the Dockyard. He organised schools, clubs, a gymnasium, and kept open house at his own home for any drunk, down-and-out or prostitute who sought shelter or a meal, day or night. He was also a ritualist, a committed Anglo-Catholic of even more extreme views than Shutte. At his services — five a day, and eight on Sundays — he insisted on candles, incense, rich vestments, music; he said Masses for the dead, and even exhorted the members of his congregation to come to him for confession.

A debate between Dolling and Doyle would have been worth paying quite a bit of money to attend, but so far as is known they did not collide publicly. Their connection arises more indirectly. In the space of less than ten years Dolling had succeeded in raising enough money, or the promise of it, to build a whole new church for himself. The foundation stone was laid on 27 October 1895, and St Agatha's was consecrated exactly a year later. Though on the outside it was mostly plain brick and rather heavy-looking, the new church's interior — which was not finally completed until 1904 — was to be as opulent and impressive as the artistry of man could devise and the finances would allow, with pillars of marble and alabaster, rich frescoes, mosaics, elaborate carvings and even a marble baldachino over the altar. As architect to design and oversee this grand project Dolling chose none other than Henry Ball, an Anglo-Catholic like himself and therefore greatly in sympathy with his ideas. Ball already had one public building to his name, the Coppersmiths' Arms in Lake Road, but now he had a far grander task to tackle, and it must surely be the demands which this prestigious commission made upon his time and energy

Saint Agatha's Church, erected in 1895/6 to the design of Conan Doyle's architect friend, Henry Ball.
(Photo: R.F. Reynolds. Cosham).

which caused him to give less attention than he might have done to the job at Hindhead. Perhaps after all it is not the builders whom we should blame for the lack of progress which had been made at Undershaw by May 1896.

Time passes. Things change. Undershaw is now a pleasant country hotel, where the proprietors will always lend a ready ear to any enquiries about its illustrious former owner. St Agatha's escaped serious damage in the bombing but was swallowed up by the wall of the expanding Dockyard, and is now reduced to the indignity of an Admiralty storehouse.

At any event, Dr Doyle had no alternative but to move his family into some temporary accommodation and wait until his house, which he had already decided to call Undershaw, from its position below a small wood, was ready. He took a furnished house, Greywood Beeches, at nearby Haslemere. Louise did not seem to mind. Anything her husband arranged was all right with her, and she would have her children with her still. In any case, the new house was probably going to be a bit too grand for her in her weakened state. But he himself could not settle. He could neither relax nor work satisfactorily under these makeshift conditions, and to go across to Hindhead and watch the workmen every day would only make him still more impatient. At least Haslemere had the advantage of being on the main line from

181

The successful author and public man. Dr Conan Doyle after he had left Southsea and taken up
residence in his newly built mansion 'Undershaw' at Hindhead.

(Photo: The Stanley Mackenzie Collection, London).

London to Portsmouth. Would she mind if he popped down to Southsea for a week or two, to look up old friends, perhaps play a bit of cricket, and work at that new book which was proving so troublesome? Why of course not, dear. You must go as soon as you like. Do let me know how are the Fords, and Mrs Claremont, and that nice Scottish doctor. And so, to come back to the main point of the story, we find from the guest lists published in the Portsmouth papers of Saturday, 16 May 1896, that Dr Conan Doyle has taken up temporary residence at No.4, Southsea Terrace.

Southsea Terrace is a substantial apartment block at the western end of the sea front. It was put up around 1870 and virtually completely refurbished in the 1980s. Each of its eleven staircases opens on to a basement

Southsea Terrace, seen undergoing refurbishment and modernisation in 1985. Dr Conan Doyle stayed at No 4, fourth from the left, in the summer of 1896.

and four upper floors having unimpeded views over the Common and Spithead to the Isle of Wight. For two weeks Conan Doyle's neighbours in the other flats at No.4 were a Mr Dean, a Mr Nicholson, and a Mr Baker and his family. Then on 30 May the guest lists show a Miss Doyle and a Miss Hawkins occupying separate apartments on the same staircase. Perhaps Lottie and Louise's sister had joined him to enjoy the south coast air and act as hostesses for him, for it is certain that he would now want to be able to return any hospitality he had received in a manner becoming to his position and reputation. On Saturday 4 July their names were absent from the lists, and the *Portsmouth Times* reported that Dr Doyle had returned to Haslemere on the Wednesday.

So for six weeks Dr Conan Doyle, the one-time local practitioner and would-be ophthalmic specialist but now the rich and famous author, inventor of the most celebrated character in all detective fiction, enjoyed the society of his old friends, played a few games of cricket, fulfilled a couple of speaking engagements in London, and worked at his latest novel. There might be no point at all in recording this interlude in his career, but for a couple of curious incidents.

Only three days before the end of his holiday, Conan Doyle bought a house in Southsea. Nothing very strange in this, perhaps, but the

South View Lodge, No 53 Kent Road, which was purchased by Conan Doyle in June, 1896, and was for some years the home of Dr Arthur Vernon Ford, the eye specialist.

curious incident, as Sherlock Holmes might say, was that he never lived in it. The title deeds now held in Portsmouth Record Office show that on 28 June, 1896 (a Sunday) the smart villa at 53 Kent Road, known as South View Lodge, was conveyed from the then owner, a Mr H.C. Connolly, to Arthur Conan Doyle MD, physician, for the sum of £1,800. The following day Dr Doyle took out a mortgage on it for £500. Five years later, in June 1901, he redeemed this. There is then an agreement dated July 1912 showing that the owner, his status then more grandly designated as "knight", let it to a Mr Percy Roberts at £83 a year: and finally a conveyance of 1919 detailing its sale to a Dr J.A. Valentine of Southsea, for £1,900.

Now why should Dr Doyle have taken this sudden decision — for it seems to have been a sudden one, since the deal was closed on a Sunday — to buy a house in Southsea, however desirable, when all his attention and, we must suppose, much of his spare capital, was being concentrated on his grand new mansion at Hindhead? Did he seriously contemplate returning permanently to Portsmouth at some time in the future? There is no evidence of this. Was it as an investment? This too seems unlikely. Property values then did not escalate in the way they sometimes do now, as is shown by the price he got for it in 1919, and a rental income of £80 a year or so would not have been a very significant factor in his finances. The explanation may be that it was simply his way of doing a good turn for an old friend.

The tenant of South View Lodge, as we have seen, was Arthur Vernon Ford, the eye surgeon, and he continued to live there until well into the 1900s, when he moved again to Outram Road, Southsea. It is known that from time to time Dr Ford was in financial difficulties. He had three sons and three daughters to educate. He had already borrowed money from his father to help establish his medical practice, and maybe also previously for his own specialist training, and these loans (no doubt with interest added) were the subject of dispute between himself and his solicitor brothers when their father's estate came to be divided up after his death in 1900. What exactly may have been Dr Ford's problems in the middle of 1896 we do not know, but it would have been entirely characteristic of Dr Doyle's impulsively generous nature to assist in providing him with a secure home and base for his practice had this actually been in jeopardy at the time.

The other curious incident takes us, I fear, even farther into the realm of speculation. The Hindhead air proved to be as good for Louise as Grant Allen had said it would. It gave her another ten years of life; she just gradually declined, and passed away peacefully in July 1906. For practically the whole of this time her husband was self-confessedly in love with another woman. She was Miss Jean Leckie, the daughter of a wealthy Scottish merchant then living in Blackheath, London S.E. In the spring of 1897, less than a year after coming back from Egypt, Conan Doyle wrote to his mother — still, even then, his confidante — to explain his feelings for Miss Leckie. True to his principles ("There is a moral sense within us which guides the agnostic as well as the Christian. . .") he kept the affair strictly platonic, and did not marry Jean until September 1907. Where or when they first met we do not know but if we turn again to the Southsea guest lists for the summer of 1896, we find that in the weeks ending 2 May, 9 May and 16 May a Mrs and Miss Leckie were staying at the Grosvenor Hotel. The red-brick Grosvenor, at which both Boulnois and Conan Doyle had been dined out, stood less than a couple of hundred yards away from Southsea Terrace across a corner of the Common. Unfortunately the newspapers do not include the Grosvenor in their lists either before or after the weeks mentioned, so the exact duration of the Leckies' stay there is unknown. Nor, of course, do we know that these were not some entirely different Leckies. We cannot, therefore, like Holmes, eliminate all the impossibles. But there remains the intriguing possibility. . .

Conan Doyle always remained fond of Portsmouth. He never forgot the scene of his early struggles and his first successes. Writing about Portsmouth in his autobiography as late as 1924 he said:

> "With its imperial associations it is a glorious place, and even now if I had to live in a town outside London it is surely to Southsea, the residential quarter of Portsmouth, that I would turn".

The old city has sheltered a number of great literary names in their day — Dickens, Meredith, Wells — but none, with the possible exception of Walter Besant, has had as close an association with it as Arthur Conan Doyle. He began his career here, and established himself not only as a reliable and sympathetic doctor but also as an outstanding local personality. He was a founder member of both Portsmouth Football Club and Portsmouth Cricket Club. During his eight years in the town he may be said to have come of age as a writer, and also to have cemented the foundations of his personal moral philosophy. He invented his most famous character here, and met his first wife here. Let it remain a pleasant speculation that he may even have met his second wife in Southsea, too.

Another view of Henry Ball's church, St Agatha's (see p. 181).

Another corner of the Canoe Lake, Craneswater, Southsea. The monument is to Alderman Emanuel Emanuel, the first Jewish mayor of Portsmouth.

Highbury Street, Old Portsmouth. Is this where Dr Doyle found his first lodgings?

St. Vincent Lodge, Kent Road, Southsea. Former home of the Rev. Desmond, one of Dr Doyle's many literary friends.

Annesley House, Southsea. One of the architect Thomas Owen's spacious villas.

Index